NATIONAL INDEX OF PARISH REGISTERS

VOLUME 10

PART 1

CHESHIRE

Compiled by
Cliff Webb, M.A., F.S.G.

SOCIETY OF GENEALOGISTS

Published by
Society of Genealogists
14 Charterhouse Buildings
Goswell Road,
London EC1M 7BA
1995

ISBN 1 85951 008 6

Volumes of the National Index of Parish Registers already published

Volume 1	General Sources of Births, Marriages and Deaths before 1837. Parish Registers, Marriage Licences, Monumental Inscriptions, Newspapers, Clandestine Marriages, Divorce, Mediaeval Sources, Other Records. General Bibliography
Volume 2	Sources for Nonconformist Genealogy and Family History. The Three Denominations (Presbyterians, Independents and Baptists). Society of Friends, Moravians, Methodists, Foreign Churches. Other Denominations.
Volume 3	Sources for Roman Catholic Genealogy and Family History. With a short section on Jewish Records contributed by Edgar Samuel. Index to Volumes 1, 2 and 3.
Volume 4	South East England. Kent, Surrey and Sussex (a revised edition of Surrey has appeared as Volume 4 Part 1 of the series).
Volume 5	South Midlands and Welsh Border. Gloucestershire, Herefordshire, Oxfordshire, Shropshire, Warwickshire, Worcestershire.
Volume 6	North and East Midlands. Part 1: Staffordshire. Part 2: Nottinghamshire. Part 3: Leicestershire and Rutland; Part 4: Derbyshire
Volume 7	East Anglia. Cambridgeshire, Norfolk, Suffolk.
Volume 8	The West of England. Part 1: Berkshire. Part 2: Wiltshire.
Volume 9	Home Counties (North of the Thames) and South East Midlands. Part 1: Bedfordshire, Huntingdonshire. Part 2: Northamptonshire. Part 3: Buckinghamshire. Part 4: Essex. Part 5: London and Middlesex
Volume 11	North East England. Part 1: Durham, Northumberland.
Volume 12	Sources for Scottish Genealogy and Family History. Historical background. Parish Registers, Ancillary Sources. Nonconformists. Bibliography.
[Volume 13]	Parish Registers of Wales.
[Volume 14]	Nonconformist Registers of Wales.

Volume 10

Part 1

CHESHIRE

ABBREVIATIONS

Add Ms	Additional Manuscripts: British Library
b	built
B	Burials
BL	Department of Manuscripts, The British Library, Great Russell St., London WC1B 3DG. A reader's ticket is necessary
Boyd	Marriage Index by P.Boyd. Copies at GL, SG and SLC. see NIPR Vol. 1
BT	Bishop's transcripts. For convenience this abbreviation is used for any annual register copy sent to an ecclesiastical superior
c	circa
C	Baptisms (also used for adult Baptisms of Baptists)
Ch Sec	Church or Chapel Secretary
C of A	College of Arms, Queen Victoria Street, London EC4V 4BT. The Library is not open to the public
Cop	Modern copies
Chester RO	Chester City Record Office
CMI	Cheshire Marriage Index
CRO	Cheshire Record Office
CRS	Catholic Record Society publications
D	Deaths
Extr	Extracts
f	founded
FHS	Family History Society
fl	flourished
I	Indexed
Inc	Incumbent
K	Kelly's Directory (+ date)
M	Marriages
MCMI	Mid Cheshire Marriage Index
Mf	Microfilm or microfiche
M Lic	Marriage Licences
Ms	Manuscript
NCMI	North Cheshire Marriage Index
NIPR	*National Index of Parish Registers*
OR	Original Register
Phil Ms	Manuscript copies of parish registers in the possession of Phillimore and Co.Ltd, Shopwyke Manor Barn, Chichester, West Sussex PO20 6BG. A fee is normally charged
PRO	The Public Record Office, Chancery Lane, London WC2A 1LR (as at 1995). From 1995/96: The Public Record Office, Ruskin Avenue, Kew, Richmond, Surrey TW9 4DK. A reader's ticket is necessary
PRS	Parish Register Society
Ptd	Printed
reb	rebuilt
SG	Society of Genealogists, 14 Charterhouse Buildings, Goswell Road, London EC1M 7BA. The Library is open to non-members on payment of hourly, half-daily and daily fees
Slater 1890	Slater's Directory, 1890
SLC	The Genealogical Society of Utah, 35 North West Temple Street, Salt Lake City, Utah 84150, U.S.A.
Ts	Typescript
Z	Births
+	Onwards. Invariably means 'until after 1837', and in the case of OR normally indicates that they continue to the present

CHESHIRE

THE COUNTY OF CHESHIRE

Cheshire is in the north-west of England. The ancient county was bounded on the north by the River Mersey (dividing it from Lancashire) and by a small part of Yorkshire, on the east by Derbyshire, the south-east by Staffordshire, the south by Shropshire, the south-west by Denbighshire and on the west by Flintshire. The length from north to south was about 32 miles and it had a breadth from east to west of about 50 miles. The original area of the county was 657,950 acres.

As usual, there have been various changes of the county boundaries. For example, the parish of Taxal was transferred to Derbyshire in 1936. Though not itself containing any large cities, Cheshire was close to two of England's most important centres of population, Liverpool and Manchester. Liverpool separated from the Wirral peninsula by the Mersey estuary was a major trade centre, and, once tunnels had been constructed under the Mersey in the nineteenth century, some Cheshire towns such as Birkinhead became effectively suburbs of Liverpool. Similarly, Manchester gradually grew to encompass the Cheshire parishes which were to its immediate south, such as Altrincham, Cheadle, Stockport and Ashton on Mersey. The development of the Manchester Ship Canal, linking Manchester to the sea ensured a considerable degree of industrialisation of what had been a mainly rural county.

Eventually, in the mid twentieth century, administrative changes were made reflecting these changes and parts of Cheshire were absorbed into the new counties of Greater Manchester and Merseyside. These do not in general affect the older records, though some nonconformist records have been deposited in Manchester Library, and rather more in Stockport Library. A part of south Lancashire including the towns of Warrington and Widnes was at the same time (1974) incorporated into Cheshire. In most cases, where deposited, Anglican registers from this area have come into the Cheshire Record Office. However, only brief notes of the parishes and chapels concerned have been given here, their records will be treated in the National Index volume for Lancashire.

The population of the administrative county was 192,305 in 1801, 334,391 in 1831, 455,725 in 1851, 644,037 in 1881 and 1,025,724 in 1921.

ECCLESIASTICAL DIVISIONS

The diocese of Chester was created in 1541, out of the dioceses of York and Lichfield and Coventry. The diocese covered not just Cheshire, but all Lancashire and parts of Yorkshire, Cumberland, Westmorland and North Wales too. Later changes, such as the creation of the dioceses of Liverpool and Manchester, reduced the diocese to be almost co-terminous with the ancient county.

RECORD REPOSITORIES AND LIBRARIES

Cheshire Record Office, Duke Street, Chester CH1 1RL.
Tel. 01244-602574. Monday to Friday 9.15 am to 4.45 pm.
This is the county record office and holds the vast majority of parish registers for the ancient county.

Chester City Record Office, Town Hall, Chester CH1 2HJ.
Tel. 01244-324324. Monday 9.30 am to 7.30 pm, Tuesday to Thursday 9.30 am to 5.30 pm.
This holds the records of the City of Chester. It does not hold parish registers as such, but does hold some nonconformist registers and some cemetery burial records. It also houses the library of the Cheshire Archaeological Society, which includes many register transcripts.

Merseyside Record Office, 4th Floor, Cunard Building, Pier Head, Liverpool L3 1EG.
Tel. 0151-236-8038. Monday to Friday 9 am to 1 pm, 2 pm to 4.45 pm.
This holds mainly archival material from Liverpool, but does hold some original material for the Wirral.

Local Studies Unit, Manchester Central Library, St Peter's Square, Manchester M2 5PD.
Tel. 0161-234-1980. Monday to Thursday 10 am to 8 pm, Friday and Saturday 10 am to 5 pm.
This holds a number of nonconformist registers from the area of Cheshire which later became part of Manchester, and films of a large number of Cheshire registers.

Stockport Archive Service and Stockport Local Heritage Library, Stockport Central Library, Wellington Road South, Stockport, Cheshire SK1 3RS.
Tel. 0161-474-4534. Monday to Friday 9 am to 8 pm. Saturday 9 am to 4 pm.
This holds a number of nonconformist registers from the Stockport area.

Tameside Local Studies Library, Trinity Street, Stalybridge, Cheshire SK15 2BN.
Tel. 0161-338-2708/3831. Monday to Wednesday and Friday 9 am to 7.30 pm, Saturday 9 am to 4 pm. Closed Thursday.
This holds some original material, especially nonconformist, for the Dukinfield, Hyde, Longdendale and Stalybridge areas.

Wirral Archives Service, Central Library, Borough Road, Birkenhead L41 2XB.
Tel. 0151-652-6106/7/8. Monday, Tuesday, Thursday and Friday 10 am to 8 pm. Saturday 10 am to 1 pm, 2 pm to 5 pm. Closed Wednesday.
This holds some original material, especially nonconformist, for the Birkenhead area.

Chetham's Library, Long Millgate, Manchester M3 1SB. Tel. 0161-834-7961.
This library holds a specialist collection on the history and topography of north-west England.

Church of Jesus Christ of the Latter Day Saints Family History Centre, Altrincham Road, Wythenshawe, Manchester M22 4BJ. Tel. 0161-902-9279.
This holds the IGI for the whole country, and through it films can be ordered for viewing from the vast collection at Salt Lake City.

John Rylands University Library of Manchester, Oxford Road, Manchester M13 9PP. Tel. (Main Library) 0161-275-3738; (Deansgate Library) 0161-834-5343.
This holds much manuscript material for the north-west of England, including the muniments of over twenty Cheshire families, but no original register material.

The following libraries maintain local history collections relating to their areas, but hold few or no archives:

Cheadle Library, Ashfield Road, Cheadle, Cheshire SK8 1BB. Tel. 0161-428-7169.
Chester Library, Northgate Street, Chester CH1 2EF. Tel. 01244-312935.
Congleton Library, Market Street, Congleton, Cheshire CW12 1BU. Tel. 01260-271141.
Crewe Library, Prince Albert Street, Crewe, Cheshire CW1 2DH. Tel. 01270-211123.
Ellesmere Port Library, Civic Way, Ellesmere Port, South Wirral L65 0BG. Tel. 0151-355-2286.
Frodsham Library, Rock Chapel, Main Street, Frodsham, Cheshire WA6 7AN. Tel. 01928-732775.
Knutsford Library, Brook Street, Knutsford, Cheshire WA16 8BP. Tel. 01565-632909.
Macclesfield Public Library, Jordongate, Macclesfield, Cheshire SK11 6TW. Tel. 01625-422512.
Nantwich Library, Beam Street, Nantwich, Cheshire CW5 5LY. Tel. 01270-624867.
Northwich Library, Witton Street, Northwich, Cheshire CW9 5DS. Tel. 01606-44221.
Runcorn Shopping City Library, Shopping City, Runcorn, Cheshire WA7 2PF. Tel. 01928-715351.
Trafford Local Studies Centre, Sale Library, Tatton Road, Sale, Cheshire M33 1YH. Tel. 0161-912-3013
Widnes Library, Victoria Square, Widnes, Cheshire WA8 7QY. Tel. 0151-423-4818.
Wilmslow Library, South Drive, Wilmslow, Cheshire SK9 1NW. Tel. 01625-528977.
Winsford Library, High Street, Winsford, Cheshire CW7 2AS. Tel. 01606-552065.

ORIGINAL PARISH REGISTERS

It is difficult to calculate the average starting date of Cheshire parish registers, since so many parishes had a number of chapelries, and it is hard to distinguish between chapels where early registrations are lost and chapelries where early registrations are in the mother church's registers. The assumption has been made that where there is no early surviving set of bishop's transcripts, and the registers also start late, that this reflects a chapelry which never had early, separate registers. Equally, it has been assumed (with rather more confidence) that a set of bishop's transcripts from roughly the normal starting date (i.e. the late 1500s or early 1600s) with registers beginning significantly later does imply the loss of registers which once existed. On these assumptions, the average Cheshire register starts in 1587. This is one of the earliest starting dates in the country, and the earliest in the north of England. With a good set of bishop's transcripts too, the overall survival rate of Cheshire registrations is very much above average.

Five Cheshire parishes have registers starting in 1538 (Brereton, Burton, Marbury, Shocklach and Warmingham). Two more series start before 1550 (Nantwich 1539 and Swettenham 1547). Twenty three start in the 1551-60 period. Thus of 100 entities with early bishop's transcripts, nearly a third start in 1560 or before. 39 more series start later in the sixteenth century, so nearly three quarters of Cheshire sequences start in 1600 or before. 15 start in the first half of the seventeenth century and eleven in the second half of the same century. Just five series start in 1700 or after (Thurstaston 1706, Bosley 1728, Harthill 1730, Hargrave 1744 and Overchurch 1759).

The Cheshire Record Office has secured deposits from the vast majority of ancient parishes in the county. The following parishes have not deposited all pre-1813 registers: Barthomley, Gawsworth, Church Lawton (pre-1753), Northenden, Thurstaston (burials only not deposited) and Weaverham. A number of parishes and chapelries have not deposited some or all of their registers, especially post-1813 ones.

In the parish listing, the name of the parish is followed by the name or dedication of the church or chapel, if any, the population of the area in 1831, any ecclesiastical history (such as status as a peculiar), followed by the hundred and poor law union the parish was in, together with any changes in these. The original registers are listed next, followed by the bishop's transcripts, details of any copies (printed, typescript or manuscript) and their location, and then any microform (not distinguishing between film and fiche) copies of registers.

The ancient parish is given first, followed by any daughter Anglican churches in order of foundation. Then follows a sequence of nonconformist churches and chapels, also in chronological order of foundation. With the latter, wherever possible foundation and/or building dates have been given, even when no records are known.

BISHOP'S TRANSCRIPTS

Cheshire bishop's transcripts are almost all at the Cheshire Record Office. In general Cheshire has a very good collection of bishop's transcripts. Many series start in the 1500s, eleven as early as the 1570s, 26 series in the 1580s and no less than 45 in the 1591-1600 period. A particularly large number of parishes have their first transcript for 1599 or 1600. Just thirteen parishes have transcripts starting in 1601-10, two in each of the next two decades and one in the 1630s. The pattern is for there to be many gaps, sometimes lengthy in the period up to about 1640, when they cease altogether until about 1660. Most parishes have something like twenty years surviving before the Civil War period. Two series only start in the 1660s and one in the 1670s. After about 1700, many parishes have complete or virtually complete collections into the nineteenth century. Many chapelries and daughter parishes were founded in the eighteenth and nineteenth centuries and have apparently later starts to their bishop's transcripts series.

There is one anomalous case, Cholmondeley Chapel, where twelve years in the 1601-31 period have bishop's transcripts, but where there are no early registers, nor, indeed any further bishop's transcripts before the modern registers start in 1840.

Cheshire bishop's transcripts come to an end at a wide variety of times, but on average run very late. With a very few exceptions sequences continue until at least the 1830s or 1840s. By 1850, just twenty sequences have ended. Sixteen more end in the 1850s and 23 in the 1860s. 34 sequences end in the 1870s and 38 in the 1880s. No less than 58 end in the 1891-1900 period and 29 more in 1901-10. Fourteen series end in the 1911-20 period. The last Cheshire bishop's transcripts were submitted from Burleydam (1922), Weaverham (1925), Buglawton (1928) and Over Tabley (1932). Virtually all Cheshire bishop's transcripts have been filmed.

MODERN COPIES OF PARISH REGISTERS

Printed

Many printed Cheshire registers fall in the Phillimore marriage series. Fourteen parishes had their marriages printed in this series. The editors concentrated on small parishes, in particular those whose marriages ceased in 1754. They devoted three volumes, however, to the large parish of Prestbury, without being able to carry them beyond the year 1789. The following is a list of these volumes with the parishes they cover.

Cheshire Phillimore Marriage Volumes

1 (1909) Disley 1591-1739; Marple 1656-1754; Taxal 1610-1812; Christleton 1697-1812; Gawsworth 1557-1812
2 (1910) Prestbury 1637-1731
3 (1911) Prestbury 1732-1770
4 (1912) Prestbury 1771-89
5 (1913) Alderley 1629-1837; Bosley 1729-50; Capesthorne 1722-47; Chelford 1674-1752; Marton 1563-1769; Poynton cum Worth 1723-53; Siddington 1722-83; Pott Shrigley 1685-1751; Taxal 1813-37; Marton addenda and corrigenda 1571-1720

At various times other Cheshire registers have been printed. The first would appear to be the Lancashire and Cheshire Record Society's publication of J. Croston's edition of the first Prestbury register which was printed in 1881, and at the end of that decade E.W. Bulkeley's edition of the first Stockport register appeared. The 1890s saw several Cheshire registers published. W.F. Irvine with some collaborators printed the pre-1700 registers of Bebington (1897), Bidston (1893), Eastham (1891) and Heswall (1896). A history of St Mary on the Hill, Chester (1898) also printed a transcript of the registers to 1812 by J.P. Earwaker and R.H. Morris. In the next decade there also appeared three Cheshire pre-1812 registers from the Parish Register Society, also edited by W.F. Irvine: Overchurch (PRS 33, 1900), Chester Cathedral (PRS 54, 1904) and Bruera (PRS 67, 1910). The Overchurch transcript is notable in being one of the first to utilise bishop's transcripts to augment a relatively late starting register. Two other registers were printed before the First World War: I.E. Jermyn's three volume edition of Frodsham to 1812 (1908-13) and L.M. Farrall's edition of Chester Holy Trinity (1914) which not only printed all the registers to 1837, but also used churchwarden's accounts to produce some burial entries as early as 1532. In addition, some registers had appeared in partworks. A small part of Macclesfield marriages was appearing in the Parish Magazine and *Cheshire Notes and Queries* was likewise printing some early material from Stockport, following on from the previous printed edition. More substantial works were F.C. Beazley's editions of Burton to 1725 and Birkenhead to 1812 which appeared in *Transactions of the Historical Society of Lancashire and Cheshire*, volumes 22-3 (1906-07).

As elsewhere, the First World War halted all progress in the publication of Cheshire registers. Indeed no further Cheshire registers were printed until 1955, apart from G.R. Axon's transcript of Hatherlow Chapel, Stockport in the *Transactions of the Lancashire and Cheshire Archaeological Society* for 1927.

Then, in 1955, R. Dickinson's labour of love on Gawsworth was printed by the Ancient Monuments Society. One or two similar efforts have appeared since: A. Anderson's edition of the early Bromborough register (1962) and Great Budworth Unitarian by W.R. Strachan (1982). Liverpool and South West Lancashire Family History Society have printed entries from the Baptist Chapel at

Hill Cliffe (1990). A few have also appeared in periodical publication, such as the first register of Guilden Sutton in *Cheshire Sheaf* (1963) and a few years of Stockport marriages in the *Manchester Genealogist* (1969). The *Family History Society of Cheshire Journal* has also included a few register transcripts. In general, however, there has been comparatively little in the way of a revival in Cheshire register printing as yet.

Typescript and manuscript

As in other counties, there has been much work done on copying Cheshire registers, and there are large collections of copies in the collections at the Cheshire Record Office, the Cheshire Archaeological Society (which are available at the Chester City Record Office) and the Society of Genealogists. However, compared with many counties, relatively few Cheshire parishes have yet been fully transcribed. Very early transcripts of Chester St Mary on the Hill and Chester St Bridget are in the British Library; they predate substantially the surviving registers. In a few other cases, registers have disappeared since being transcribed.

Some parishes have coverage in Boyd's Marriage Index, while a few are only to 1754, nearly half have coverage to 1812 and nearly half to 1837. Boyd's Index is to be found at the Society of Genealogists. Microfilm copies may be seen through Mormon Family History Centres.

The Cheshire Marriage Index, which has been compiled by Bertram Merrell mainly from the bishop's transcripts, is to males only, and is held in four parts: 1580-1700, 1701-55, 1756-1800 and 1801-37. The compiler's address is 3912 South 2520 West, West Valley City, Utah 84119, USA. A fee of £5 or $10 is charged for a single marriage search in each chronological section. There is a copy of the 1801-37 period for A-C only is on microfiche at the Society of Genealogists. It is believed that the rest of the index will be appearing on microfiche eventually. Parishes and periods in this index are denoted in the text by (CMI). Another Cheshire marriage index, covering mainly the north and the east of the county, and with nearly a quarter of a million entries is held by Mrs P.M. Litton, 2 Florence Road, Harrogate, North Yorkshire HG2 0LD. Mrs Litton charges £1 + SAE for a specific entry, and can extract all of a surname for members of the Guild of One-Name Studies. Parishes and periods in this index are denoted in the text by (NCMI). Mrs Litton's index also includes marriage licences 1606-1719 from the printed edition. The Mid Cheshire Marriage Index is available for a donation of £1 per marriage and SAE from C. Thomson, 15 Mayfield Grove, Cuddington, Northwich, Cheshire, CW8 2LT (denoted in the text by (MCMI)).

Microform

The Cheshire Record Office has filmed just over half of its parish register collection, and virtually all its bishop's transcripts. Copies of many of them will be found at Salt Lake City (and are thus available through Family History Centres). In addition many film copies are to be found at the Manchester Local Studies Library, and local reference libraries such as Birkenhead (now known as Wallasey Archives), Nantwich, Stockport, etc. have obtained copies of those films relative to their area of interest.

MARRIAGE LICENCES, ALLEGATIONS AND BONDS

Allegations and bonds for marriage licences for the diocese of Chester are at Cheshire Record Office. Act Books survive from 1605, and these have been abstracted and published to 1700 by the Lancashire and Cheshire Record Society. From 1661, the original bonds and allegations survive in chronological order. Again the Lancashire and Cheshire Record Society have abstracted and published them for the period 1701-19. From 1716, the bonds and allegations are, within each year, arranged by alphabetical order of groom's name. Bonds for 1776 (A-L only) were published by the Family History Society of Cheshire in their *Journal* in the mid-1970s.

In addition, Cheshire couples could get a licence to marry from the Archbishop of York, or from the Faculty Office of the Archbishop of Canterbury. For details of these records see Jeremy Gibson's *Bishops' Transcripts and Marriage Licences, Bonds and Allegations: A Guide to their Location and Indexes* (3rd edition, Federation of Family History Societies, 1991).

NONCONFORMISTS

ROMAN CATHOLICS

After England was divided into districts in 1688, Cheshire was in the North-West District. With the re-establishment of Roman Catholic dioceses, it became part of the Diocese of Shrewsbury. Full details of Roman Catholic registers in Cheshire appear in Michael Gandy's *Catholic Missions and Registers 1700-1880* Volume 5 (1993).

SOCIETY OF FRIENDS (QUAKERS)

Cheshire Quakers were part of the Cheshire Quarterly Meeting 1668-1783, Cheshire and Staffordshire Quarterly Meeting 1783-1854 and Lancashire and Cheshire Quarterly Meeting from 1854. Monthly meetings were organised at various times based on Chester, Frandley, Morley and Nantwich.

The Cheshire Record Office has microfilm copies of the Quarterly Meeting registers, the originals of which are at the Public Record Office. A list of these records follows:

Cheshire Quarterly Meeting (from 1783 Cheshire and Staffordshire Quarterly Meeting):

Z 1648-1783, M 1667-1765, B 1655-1782 (PRO: RG 6/1031, 1035, 1037, 1256)

Z 1783-1836, M 1768-1837, B 1783-1837 (PRO: RG 6/180, 285-288, 294, 297, 303)

Morley Monthly Meeting later Cheshire Monthly Meeting:

Z 1654-1830, M 1654-1831, B 1654-1776 (PRO: RG 6/96, 157, 181, 213, 1036, 1398)

Mobberley Monthly Meeting:

B 1655-1742 (PRO: RG 6/1603)

Congleton Monthly Meeting:

B 1668-1831 (PRO: RG 6/97-98, 214, 1329)

Nantwich Monthly Meeting:

Z 1776-93, M 1776-89, B 1776-94 (PRO: RG 6/156, 254-255)

Frandley and Nantwich Monthly Meeting:

Z 1795-1837, M 1802-37, B 1795-1837 (PRO: RG 6/182, 215-216)

Monthly Meeting of Cheshire:

Z 1776-99, 1833-37, M 1831-37, B 1831-37 (PRO: RG 6/256)

From 1802 to 1837 Runcorn, Great Budworth and Latchford (in Grappenhall) were in Lancashire Quarterly Meeting. From 1831 to 1837 Birkenhead, Southport Chester and Wallasey were also in Lancashire Quarterly Meeting. Registers at the Public Record Office for this period are:

Lancashire Quarterly Meeting:

Z 1796-1837, M 1795-1837, B 1799-1837 (PRO: RG 6/376, 639-642, 644-645, 1005, 1007-1008, 1041-1044, 1096, 1156)

Hardshaw West Monthly Meeting:

Z 1798-1836, M 1798-1837, B 1798-1838 (PRO: RG 6/380, 528, 1529-1530, 1564)

Copies of all these registers are also held at the Library of the Religious Society of Friends, Friends House, Euston Road, London NW1 2BJ.

INDEPENDENTS

Several Cheshire Independent chapels date from the Restoration period. However, some of these surrendered no registers and no seventeenth century registers appear to survive. The earliest Cheshire Independent register is Stockport (1709) followed by Hatherlow (1732) and Tintwistle (1747). Registers starting in the late eighteenth century survive for Marple Bridge (1761), Gatley (1779), Macclesfield (1775), Congleton (1785), Stockport (another) (1788), Tattenhall (1798), Sandbach (1799) and Ashton upon Mersey (1799). Surrendered or otherwise deposited registers start in the 1800-1837 period for seventeen further chapels, some founded nearly two hundred years before.

BAPTISTS

Baptists were not strong in Cheshire, most chapels being in the east of the county. No very early Baptist chapels survive in Cheshire apart from Hill Cliffe. Five pre-1837 foundations surrendered registers, the earliest being Great Warford, Alderley (1757). Others were Nantwich (1800), Tarporley (1801), Stalybridge Particular (1807) and Stalybridge General (1809). Towns generally had a Baptist chapel by the mid-nineteenth century.

PRESBYTERIANS AND UNITARIANS

As elsewhere, most seventeenth-century chapels calling themselves Presbyterian became Unitarian during the eighteenth and early nineteenth centuries. Registers were surrendered from Stockport (1710), Chester (1713), Macclesfield (1713), Stockport (another) (1761), Great Budworth (1779), Nantwich (1783), Knutsford (1792), Congleton (1814) and Wilmslow (Styal) (1833). Wilmslow's Dean Row Chapel's registers dating from 1749 are at the Cheshire Record Office.

METHODISTS

Methodism grew rapidly in Cheshire; the first meetings were in private homes, but chapels were built from 1759. At first, however, all registrations remained in the parish church, and only towards the end of the eighteenth century do any Methodist registers begin, and then generally only baptismal records. Virtually no Methodist marriage registers were kept until 1898, and at no time have Methodists had many burial grounds. As in other counties, however, most Cheshire townships and villages had one or more Methodist chapels by the end of the nineteenth century. Methodist registers, therefore, are much fewer than chapels.

Nonetheless thirty Wesleyan Methodist registers are known which start in 1837 or earlier, the earliest being Stockport (1793). In addition there are six Primitive Methodist chapels, six Methodist New Connexion (later United Methodist), two Calvinist Methodist, two Independent Methodist and two Lady Huntingdon's Connexion chapels with registers predating 1837 are known.

Most of these registers were surrendered in 1837 and are at the Public Record Office, London. They have been filmed by the Genealogical Society of Utah, and are available at the Cheshire Record Office and through Mormon Family History Centres.

MORAVIAN

There was a Moravian chapel at Dukinfield, founded in 1724 and a register was surrendered dating from 1785.

MONUMENTAL INSCRIPTIONS

There are large collections of copies at both the Cheshire Record Office and the Society of Genealogists. The various Cheshire family history societies all have active copying programmes and no attempt has been made to indicate coverage of monumental inscriptions in this volume.

NEWSPAPERS

For a straightforward guide and location list reference should be made to *Local Newspapers 1750-1920* compiled J.S.W. Gibson, Federation of Family History Societies, 1991.

REGIMENTS

The most likely regiment for Cheshire men was the twenty-second or Cheshire Regiment. A history of the regiment appears in W.H. Anderson's *A History of the Twenty-Second Cheshire Regiment* 1689-1849 (1920).

PUBLISHING SOCIETIES AND BIBLIOGRAPHY

There are three family history societies in Cheshire: The Family History Society of Cheshire (founded 1969), North Cheshire Family History Society (founded 1977) and South Cheshire Family History Society (founded 1990, formerly the Nantwich Group of the Family History Society of Cheshire). All have extensive programmes for copying material, especially monumental inscriptions. It should also not be forgotten that with the absorption of parts of Cheshire into the cities of Liverpool and Manchester, the Liverpool and South West Lancashire Family History Society and the Manchester and Lancashire Family History Society may have material of interest to the Cheshire genealogist. The 72 volumes of the *Cheshire Sheaf* printed a vast amount of miscellaneous genealogical source material.

Two record publishing societies operate in Cheshire, both covering Lancashire as well. The Chetham Society and the Lancashire and Cheshire Record Society both print texts and indexes to records of interest in the county. In addition the Historic Society of Lancashire and Cheshire and the Lancashire and Cheshire Antiquarian Society have each printed Transactions and the Chester Archaeological and Historic Society has printed a journal, each with much useful genealogical material.

A full genealogical bibliography of Cheshire in two volumes has recently been published in Stuart Raymond's series of county bibliographies, published by the Federation of Family History Societies, so no attempt has been made to compile one here.

ACTON St Mary (3,928) [part Nantwich Borough, part Nantwich Hundred; Nantwich Union]
OR C 1653-1859, M 1653-1858, Banns 1789-1967, B 1653-1882 (CRO)
BT 1586, 1589, 1593, 1599-1600, 1605, 1609, 1611-14, 1617-18, 1620-24, 1626, 1628, 1630-33, 1636-37, 1639, 1663-69, 1671-82, 1684-1827, 1829-86 (+ index CB 1873-76) (CRO)
Cop C 1653-1812, M 1653-1754, B 1653-1750 (Ts CRO, SG); M 1672-1754 (NCMI); M 1689-1708, 1750-1837 (CMI)
Cop (Mf) C 1653-1859, M 1653-1858, B 1653-1882 (CRO, Manchester Local Hist Lib)

ACTON Faddiley (Wesleyan Methodist) b 1809, reb 1873, closed 1980
OR M 1899-1937 (CRO)

ACTON Burland (Primitive Methodist) b 1833, closed 1965
OR ZC 1826-37 (PRO: RG 4/574)
Cop (Mf) ZC 1826-37 (CRO, SLC)

ACTON Cholmondeston Chapel (Wesleyan Methodist) f before 1850, closed 1972
OR M 1914-69 (CRO)

ACTON Coole Pilate (United Methodist) b 1850 (K 1939)

ACTON Edleston (Primitive Methodist) b 1855 (K 1939)

ACTON Brindley (Wesleyan Methodist) b 1873 (K 1939)

ACTON Sound Heath Chapel (Primitive Methodist) b 1875

ACTON Ravensmoor, Burland (Wesleyan Methodist) b 1878 (K 1939)

ACTON also township in Weaverham (335)

ACTON GRANGE township in Runcorn (Daresbury chapelry) (149)

ADLINGTON chapelry in Prestbury (1,066)

AGDEN chapelry in Malpas (104)

AGDEN township part in Rosthern, chiefly in Bowdon (99)

ALDERLEY St Mary (1,338) [Macclesfield Hundred; Macclesfield Union]
OR C 1629-1894, M 1629-1901, B 1629-1941 (CRO)
BT 1599-1600, 1612, 1615, 1620-21, 1623-24, 1626-28, 1630-31, 1633-37, 1639-41, 1658-85, 1687-92, 1694, 1696-1749, 1751-56, 1758-1837 (CRO)
Cop M 1629-1837 (Ptd, Phil 5, 1913); M 1629-1837 (Boyd, NCMI); M 1728-1837 (CMI)
Cop (Mf) C 1629-1894, M 1629-1901, B 1629-1941 (CRO, Manchester Local Hist Lib)

ALDERLEY Great Warford (Baptist) (Lewis 1831) (K 1939)
OR Z 1757+, B 1800-59, 1880+ (Ch Sec)
Cop Z 1757-1854, B 1800-59, 1880-1929 (SG)

ALDERLEY Great Warford (Methodist) b 1843, closed 1963
OR C 1859-1961 (CRO)

ALDERLEY EDGE St Phillip *see* **CHORLEY St Phillip**

ALDERSEY township in Coddington

ALDFORD St John the Baptist (1,710) [Broxford Hundred; Great Boughton Union 1837-71, Tarvin Union 1871-1930]
OR C 1639-1919, M 1641-1835, Banns 1754-1812, B 1639-1858 (CRO)
BT 1599, 1604-05, 1610, 1613-14, 1617-18, 1620, 1622-29, 1641, 1662, 1664, 1666-72, 1674, 1676-77, 1679-85, 1690-91, 1694, 1696-97, 1699, 1701-1826, 1829-38, 1840-41, 1843-45, 1847-54, 1856-57, 1862-1901, 1913-15 (+ index CB 1873-93) (CRO)
Cop M 1756-1837 (CMI)
Cop (Mf) C 1639-1919, M 1641-1835, B 1639-1858 (CRO, Manchester Local Hist Lib)

ALDFORD (United Methodist) f 1883, b 1891, closed 1979
OR C 1963-74 (Chester RO)

ALLOSTOCK township in Great Budworth (448)

ALPRAHAM township in Bunbury (418)

ALSAGER Christ Church (446) township in Bartholmey, part in Staffordshire until 1866 [Nantwich Hundred; Congleton Union]
OR C 1789-1889, M 1852-68, B 1789-1908 (CRO)
BT 1789-1801, 1813-18, 1820-42 (CRO)
Cop C 1789-1889, M 1852-68, B 1789-1908 (Ts CRO)

ALSAGER St Mary Magdalen b 1894
OR CMB 1881+ (Inc)

ALSAGER Chapel Lane Chapel, Hassall Road (Wesleyan Methodist) b 1834, reb 1852, *fl.*1968

ALSAGER Crewe Road Chapel (Primitive Methodist) b 1862, closed 1969
OR C 1863-1967 (CRO)

ALSAGER Wesley Place Chapel, Lawton Road (Wesleyan Methodist) b 1869

ALSAGER Brookhouse Road (Independent, later United Reformed Church) f 1877, *fl.*1991

ALSAGER St Gabriel, Lawton Road (Roman Catholic) b 1955

ALTRINCHAM Board of Guardians
OR D 1898-1940 (CRO)

ALTRINCHAM St George (2,708) chapel b 1799, and borough in Bowdon, made parochial in 1812 [Bucklow Hundred; Altrincham Borough Union]
OR C 1799-1962, M 1861-1951, B 1800-1926 (CRO)
BT 1814-57, 1859-77, 1893-95, 1898 (+ index CB 1873-77, 1893) (CRO)
Cop (Mf) C 1799-1907, M 1861-1913 (CRO)

ALTRINCHAM St John the Evangelist (created from Bowdon, Dunham Massey and Timperley, 1867)
OR C 1866-1949, M 1867-1984, Banns 1867-1901, 1972-87 (CRO)
BT C 1867-1900 (+ index C 1873-93) (CRO)
Cop (Mf) C 1866-1900, M 1867-1905, 1961-84 (CRO)

ALTRINCHAM Chapel Walk (Wesleyan Methodist) f 1795 (Lewis 1831) (White 1860)
OR ZC 1796-37 (PRO: RG 4/156-57)
Cop (Mf) ZC 1796-37 (CRO, SLC)

ALTRINCHAM George Street (Methodist New Connexion, later United Methodist) f 1817, b 1821 (Slater 1890)
OR ZC 1819-37 (PRO: RG 4/158)
Cop (Mf) ZC 1819-37 (CRO, SLC)

ALTRINCHAM Dunham Road (Unitarian) (Lewis 1831) (Slater 1890)

ALTRINCHAM Bowdon Downs (Independent) f 1839
OR C 1840-1969, M 1846-63, 1876-1972 (Manchester Local Hist Lib)

ALTRINCHAM Timperley (Wesleyan Methodist) b 1843 (Slater 1890)

ALTRINCHAM St Vincent de Paul, Bentlinck Road (Roman Catholic) f 1847

ALTRINCHAM The Downs (Independent) b 1848 (Slater 1890)

ALTRINCHAM Oxford Road (Primitive Methodist) b 1858 (Slater 1890)

ALTRINCHAM Woodlands Road (Bank Street) (Wesleyan Methodist) b 1866 (Slater 1890)

ALTRINCHAM Baguley (Independent) *fl.* 1868 (Slater 1890)

ALTRINCHAM Hale (Warburton Green) (Unitarian) *fl.* 1872 (Slater 1890)

ALTRINCHAM Hale Road (Baptist) f 1872, *fl.* 1989

ALTRINCHAM Baguley (Baptist) *fl.* 1878 (Slater 1890)

ALTRINCHAM Railway Street (Baptist) (Slater 1890)

ALTRINCHAM Shaw's Lane (Salvation Army) (Slater 1890)

ALTRINCHAM George Street (Bible Christian) (Slater 1890)

ALTRINCHAM Lloyd Street (Christian Brethren) (Slater 1890)

ALTRINCHAM Trinity, Delamer Road, Bowdon (Presbyterian) (Slater 1890)

ALTRINCHAM Dunham Woodhouses (Wesleyan Methodist) (Slater 1890)

ALTRINCHAM Enville Road, Bowdon (Wesleyan Methodist) (Slater 1890)

ALTRINCHAM Baguley (Wesleyan Methodist) (Slater 1890)

ALTRINCHAM Henry Street, Hale (Wesleyan Methodist) (Slater 1890)

ALTRINCHAM Sinderland (Wesleyan Methodist) (Slater 1890)

ALTRINCHAM Navigation Road, Broadheath (Independent) (Slater 1890)

ALTRINCHAM Oxford Road (Independent) (Slater 1890)

ALTRINCHAM St Hugh of Lincoln, Manchester Road (Roman Catholic) f 1930

ALTRINCHAM St John the Baptist, Thorley Lane (Roman Catholic) f 1957

ALTRINCHAM Holy Angels, Hale Barns (Roman Catholic) f 1958

ALVANLEY St John the Evangelist (346) chapelry in Frodsham, created a parish in 1741 [Eddisbury Hundred; Runcorn Union]
OR C 1809-1970, Banns 1861-1953, B 1791-1885 (CRO); M 1861+ (Inc)
BT 1811-46, 1848-68, 1873-77 (+ index CB 1873-77) (CRO)
Cop (Mf) C 1809-1970, B 1791-1885 (CRO, Manchester Local Hist Lib)

ALVASTON township in Nantwich (41)

ANDERTON township in Great Budworth (327)

ANTROBUS St Mark (476) township in Great Budworth, created a parish in 1848
OR C 1848-1920, M 1848-1983, B 1848-1974 (CRO)
Cop M 1848-1900 (MCMI)

ANTROBUS (Wesleyan Methodist) reb 1935 (K 1928-39)

ANTROBUS Meeting House, Seven Oaks (Society of Friends) f 17th century (K 1928-39)
OR see Cheshire Quaker Registers

APPLETON township in Great Budworth

APPLETON (Methodist) (K 1939)

APPLETON Hill Cliff (Baptist) f 1633, b 1840 (K 1939)
OR Records 1633-1987, but no registers (CRO)
Cop Z 1783-1837, B 1802-39 (Ptd, Liverpool and S.W. Lancashire FHS, 1990)

APPLETON THORN St Cross (created from Stretton, 1887)
OR CMB 1887+ (Inc)

ARCLID township in Sandbach (79)

ARROWE township in Woodchurch (91)

ASHLEY St Elizabeth (379) township in Bowdon, created a parish in 1881
OR C 1880-1969 (CRO); MB 1880+ (Inc)
BT 1885-89, 1909 (+ index C 1880-85) (CRO)

ASHTON HAYES St John the Evangelist (405) township in Tarvin, created a parish in 1849
OR C 1849-1952, M 1849-1983, Banns 1849-1986, B 1849-1926 (CRO)
BT 1849-1900 (CRO)

ASHTON HAYES (Wesleyan Methodist) b 1845, reb 1888 (K 1939)

ASHTON HAYES Mouldsworth (Wesleyan Methodist) b 1877 (K 1939)

ASHTON upon MERSEY St Martin (2,078) [Bucklow Hundred; Altrincham Union]
OR C 1636-1880, M 1636-1888, Banns 1914-40, B 1636-1890 (CRO)
BT 1605, 1607, 1619?, 1630, 1632-33, 1635-37, 1658-60, c1661, 1663, 1666, 1668-72, 1674-76, 1679-82, 1684, 1692-97, 1701-02, 1704-11, 1713, 1715-1805, 1807-76 (+ index CB 1873-76) (CRO)
Cop M 1605-1837 (NCMI); M 1636-61, 1756-1837 (CMI)
Cop (Mf) C 1636-1880, M 1636-1888, B 1636-1890 (CRO, Manchester Local Hist Lib)

ASHTON upon MERSEY St Mary Magdalene (created from Ashton upon Mersey St Martin, 1894)
OR CMB 1874+ (Inc)
BT (index C 1874-76) (CRO)

ASHTON upon MERSEY Meeting House (Society of Friends)
OR see Cheshire Quaker Registers
BT B 1865-74 (CRO)

ASHTON upon MERSEY School Lane (Independent) f 1802 *fl.*1850
OR ZC 1799-1837 (PRO: RG 4/304)
Cop (Mf) ZC 1799-1837 (CRO, SLC)

ASHTON upon MERSEY (Calvinist) (Lewis 1831)

ASHTON upon MERSEY Sale Moor (Wesleyan Methodist) f 1820
OR ZC 1820-37 (PRO: RG 4/415)
Cop (Mf) ZC 1820-37 (CRO, SLC)

ASHTON upon MERSEY (Unitarian) (Lewis 1831)

ASTBURY St Mary (14,673) [part Northwich Hundred, part Macclesfield Hundred; Congleton Union]
OR C 1572-1953, M 1572-1969, B 1572-1970 (CRO)
BT 1593, 1596, 1600, 1604, 1607-09, 1611-15, 1617-23, 1626-27, 1629-31, 1633, 1635-37, 1639, 1657-59, 1661-62, 1664-76, 1679-80, 1682-85, 1693-97, 1702-1898 (CRO)
Cop CMB 1572-1641 (Ts CRO); C 1750-1815 (SG); M 1813-37 (NCMI); M 1814, 1834 (CMI)
Cop (Mf) C 1572-1953, M 1572-1969, B 1572-1970 (CRO, Congleton Lib, Manchester Local Hist Lib)

ASTBURY Wornish Nook Chapel (Primitive Methodist) b 1833, sold to Wesleyans, 1891, closed 1967

ASTBURY Brownlow Chapel, Newbold Astbury (Wesleyan Methodist) b 1852

ASTON by BUDWORTH township in Great Budworth

ASTON by SUTTON St Peter (166) chapelry in Runcorn, created a parish in 1861
OR C 1635-1924, M 1635-1845, Banns 1830-1909, B 1635-1928 (CRO)
BT 1623, 1635-37, 1641, 1665-66, 1671-76, 1678, 1682-85, 1687-1731, 1733-39, 1741-60, 1762-1893 (+ index CB 1873-86) (CRO)
Cop M 1701-1837 (NCMI); M 1682-1731, 1733-60, 1762-1837 (CMI)
Cop (Mf) C 1635-1924, M 1635-1845, B 1635-1928 (CRO, Manchester Local Hist Lib)

ASTON by SUTTON Sutton Weaver (Methodist) (K 1939)

ASTON GRANGE township in Runcorn (36)

ASTON juxta MONDRUM township in Acton (152)

AUDLEM Cemetery (opened 1874; 2 acres)

AUDLEM St James (2,795) [Nantwich Hundred; Nantwich Union]
OR C 1557-1928, M 1557-1923, Banns 1813-46, 1866-1924, B 1557-1947 (CRO)
BT 1579, 1600-02, 1605, 1607-10, 1612-15, 1617, 1620-21, 1626-27, 1632-33, 1636-39, 1641, 1658-68, 1670-85, 1687, 1689-1843, 1848-53, 1864-1910 (+ index CB 1873-77) (CRO)
Cop M 1753-1837 (NCMI); M 1665-73, 1799-1837 (CMI)
Cop (Mf) C 1557-1928, M 1557-1923, B 1557-1947 (CRO, Manchester Local Hist Lib)

AUDLEM (Baptist) f 1812, *fl.*1989

AUDLEM Hankelow (Wesleyan Methodist) b 1838, reb 1935, *fl.* 1945

AUDLEM (Baptist) b 1840 (K 1939)

AUDLEM (Primitive Methodist) b 1852, closed 1943

AUDLEM Jubilee Chapel, Cox Bank (Primitive Methodist) b 1861 (K 1939)

AUDLEM (Wesleyan Methodist) b 1862 (K 1939)

AUDLEM (Primitive Methodist) b 1871 (K 1939)
OR C 1878-1926 (CRO)

AUDLEM Buerton (United Free Gospel) b 1885 (K 1939)

AUDLEM Buerton (Wesleyan Methodist) b 1891, closed 1975

AUSTERSON township in Acton

BACHE township in Chester St Oswald (34)

BACKFORD St Oswald (487) [part Wirral Hundred, part Broxton Hundred; Great Boughton Union]
OR C 1562-1881, M 1562-1977, Banns 1824-1906, B 1562-1981 (CRO)
BT 1581, 1586, 1599-1600, 1602, 1604-05, 1607-10, 1613-17, 1619-24, 1626-27, 1632-34, 1636, 1638-41, 1663-64, 1669-71, 1674-77, 1679-81, 1685, 1690-91, 1694-1703, 1705-39, 1741-1826, 1828-30, 1832-40 (CRO)
Cop M 1782-1837 (CMI)
Cop (Mf) C 1562-1859, M 1562-1838, B 1562-1875 (CRO, Manchester Local Hist Lib)

BADDILEY St Michael (267) [Nantwich Hundred; Nantwich Union]
OR C 1579-1990, M 1579-1980, Banns 1808-80, 1894-1991, B 1579-1991 (CRO)
BT 1596, 1600, 1605-06, 1608-18, 1622, 1626, 1628, 1630-33, 1636-38, 1663-85, 1691-96, 1698-1732, 1734, 1737-61, 1763, 1765-1836, 1893-1905 (CRO)
Cop 1597-1741 (Nantwich Lib); M 1666-83, 1715-34, 1741-50, 1752-1837 (CMI)
Cop (Mf) CB 1579-1812, M 1579-1837

BADDILEY (Wesleyan Methodist) b 1878 (K 1939)

BADDINGTON township in Acton (132)

BAGULEY St John (468) township in Bowdon, created a parish in 1848
OR CMB 1867+ (Inc)
BT 1868-77 (+ index CB 1873-77, 1886) (CRO)

BANK QUAY Mission Church chapelry in Lancashire, transferred to Cheshire, 1974

BARNSTON Christ Church (123) township in Woodchurch, created a parish in 1870
OR C 1871-1935, Banns 1872-1937, 1966-75 (CRO); MB 1871+ (Inc)
BT 1873-83 (+ index CB 1873-83) (CRO)
Cop M 1849-1903 (MCMI)

BARNTON Christ Church (730) township in Great Budworth, created a parish in 1843
OR C 1906-86, M 1849-1991, B 1852-1926 (CRO)
BT 1855-56, 1874-96 (+ index CB 1874-93) (CRO)

BARNTON Runcorn Road (Wesleyan Methodist) f 1813, b 1875, closed 1962
OR C 1865-1941, M 1939-62 (CRO)

BARNTON Mount Tabor Chapel (United Methodist) f 1836, b 1867, closed 1969
OR M 1913-69 (CRO)

BARNTON (Primitive Methodist) b 1896 (K 1939)

BARNTON Our Lady of Fatima, Lydyett Lane (Roman Catholic) f 1953

BARROW St Bartholomew (678) [Eddisbury Hundred; Great Boughton Union]
OR C 1572-1844, M 1590-1837, Banns 1824-1907, B 1572-1921 (CRO)
BT 1596, 1600-01, 1604-05, 1607, 1609-15, 1617-18, 1622-25, 1627-30, 1635, 1637, 1639, 1664, 1666, 1668-86, 1690-92, 1694-1840, 1845-47, 1851, 1873-74, 1876-82 (+ index CB 1873-82) (CRO)
Cop 1571-1880 (Ts I CRO); C 1572-1681, M 1621-84, B 1620-62 (Chester AS); M 1590-1837 (NCMI); M 1698-1852 (CMI)

BARROW Great Barrow (Wesleyan Methodist) f 1842, closed 1981
OR C 1924-61 (Chester RO)

BARROW (United Methodist) b 1847, reb 1876, closed 1954

BARROW Little Barrow (Primitive Methodist) (K 1928-39)

BARTHOMLEY St Bertoline (2,523) [part Nantwich Hundred, part North Pirehill Hundred, Staffs; Nantwich Union]
OR C 1562-1885, M 1562-1923, Banns 1905-33, B 1562-1888 (CRO)
BT 1599, 1604-05, 1607-10, 1613-15, 1617-18, 1620-24, 1626-31, 1633, 1636-41, 1658-66, 1668-85, 1687-1864 (CRO)
Cop M 1562-1839 (Ts I CRO, SG); M 1563-1837 (NCMI); M 1687-1703, 1741-80 (CMI)

BARTINGTON township in Great Budworth (76)

BARTON township in Farndon (168)

BASFORD township in Wybunbury (85)

BATHERTON township in Wybunbury

BEBINGTON St Andrew, Lower Bebington (2,193) [Wirral Hundred; Wirral Union]
OR C 1558-1935, M 1558-1930, Banns 1785-1824, 1935-67, B 1558-1909 (CRO)
BT 1597, 1599-1600, 1604-05, 1608-10, 1613-15, 1617-24, 1626-27, 1630, 1632-34, 1636-38, 1640-42, 1660, 1666, 1668-71, 1673-76, 1679-82, 1684-85, 1690-91, 1694-1837, 1867-75, 1892-1905 (+ index B 1891, CB 1892-93) (CRO)
Cop 1558-1701 (Ptd, F. Sanders and W.F. Irvine, 1897); M 1752-1837 (CMI)
Cop (Mf) C 1558-1907, M 1558-1923, B 1558-1909 (CRO, Wirral Archives, Manchester Local Hist Lib)

BEBINGTON Bromborough Road, Lower Bebington (Wesleyan Methodist: Bebington South Circuit) b 1895, reb 1928 (K 1946)

BEBINGTON Grange Chapel, Kings Road (United Reformed Church) f 1943, *fl.* 1991

BEBINGTON, HIGHER Christ Church, King's Road township in Bebington, b 1858, created a parish in 1877
OR C 1859-1922, M 1877-1933 (CRO); B 1859+ (Inc)
BT 1893-95 (CRO)

BEBINGTON, HIGHER (Wesleyan Methodist: Bebington South Circuit) f 1903 (K 1946)

BEESTON township in Bunbury (433)

BENCHILL St Luke created from Northenden, 1936
OR CM 1936+ (Inc)

BETCHTON township in Sandbach

BEXTON township in Knutsford (76)

BICKERTON Cemetery (opened 1880; 1 acre)

BICKERTON Holy Trinity (373) township in Malpas, created a parish in 1840
OR C 1847-1960, M 1868-1975, Banns 1868-1950, B 1847-1948 (CRO)
BT 1847, 1855-1910 (+ index CB 1873-89, C 1890-92) (CRO)

BICKERTON Broxton (Primitive Methodist) (K 1928-39)

BICKERTON Bulkeley (Primitive Methodist) (K 1928-39)

BICKLEY St Winefrede township in Malpas, created a parish in 1893 from Malpas, Marbury and Wrenbury
OR C 1892-1965, M 1893-1948, graves 1893-1935 (CRO)
BT 1892-94 (CRO)

BICKLEY (Wesleyan Methodist) (Lewis 1831)

BICKLEY (Primitive Methodist) b 1882 (K 1939)

BICKLEY Chorley (Primitive Methodist) b 1873 (K 1939)

BIDSTON St Oswald (3,434) [Wirral Hundred; Wirral Union]
OR C 1682-1986, M 1682-1980, Banns 1754-1812, B 1679-1958 (CRO)
BT 1581, 1588, 1596, 1605, 1612, 1614-15, 1617-24, 1632-34, 1636, 1638-39, 1666, 1668-71, 1673, 1675-76, 1679-81, 1683-85, 1687-91, 1694-1701, 1704-13, 1715-27, 1729-39, 1741-42, 1745-1843, 1845-63 (CRO)
Cop 1581-1700 (Ptd, W.F. Irvine, 1893); 1701-60 (CRO); M 1685-1700, 1735-1836 (CMI)
Cop (Mf) C 1682-1862, M 1682-1929, B 1679-1898 (CRO)

BIRCHES township in Great Budworth (9)

BIRKENHEAD Board of Guardians
OR Z 1864-1942, C 1890-1950, M 1907-17, D 1864-1944 (Wirral Archives)

BIRKENHEAD Cemetery, Flaybrick Hill, Tollemache Road (K 1946)

BIRKENHEAD St Mary, Church Street (2,569) chapelry in Bidston, created a parish in 1738 [Wirral Hundred; Wirral Union]
OR C 1721-1968, M 1721-1974, Banns 1829-45, 1874-95, B 1719-1957 (CRO)
BT 1813-39 (CRO)
Cop 1721-1812 (Ptd, F.C. Beazley, *Transactions of Hist. Soc. of Lancashire and Cheshire* 22, 1906); M 1719-88 (SG); M 1721-35, 1756-1811, 1815-33 (CMI)
Cop (Mf) C 1721-1968, M 1721-1965, B 1719-1957 (CRO, Wirral Archives, Manchester Local Hist Lib); C 1813-44, B 1813-37 (SG)

BIRKENHEAD Holy Trinity, Price Street created a parish in 1841 from St Mary
OR C 1840-1974, M 1842-1974 (CRO)

BIRKENHEAD St Anne, Beckwith Street b 1847, created a parish in 1861 from Holy Trinity
OR C 1850-1950, M 1862-1940, Banns 1876-1978 (CRO)
BT C 1876-1915 (+ index C 1876-92) (CRO)
Cop (Mf) C 1850-1896, M 1862-1889 (CRO, Wirral Archives)

BIRKENHEAD St John the Evangelist, Grange Road, created a parish in 1859 from St Mary
OR C 1859-1971, M 1859-1968, Banns 1859-74 (CRO)
Cop (Mf) C 1859-1971, M 1859-1968 (CRO, Wirral Archives, Manchester Local Hist Lib)

BIRKENHEAD St Paul, Argyle Street, created a parish in 1862 from St Mary
OR C 1863-1948, M 1864-1948 (CRO)

BIRKENHEAD St James, Laird Street, b 1858, created a parish in 1869 from St Mary
OR C 1865-1967, M 1869-1972 (CRO)
BT C 1898-99 (CRO)
Cop (Mf) C 1865-1967, M 1869-1972 (CRO, Manchester Local Hist Lib)

BIRKENHEAD St Peter, Cathcart Street, created a parish in 1868 from Holy Trinity
OR C 1867-1983, M 1868-1968 (CRO)

BIRKENHEAD St Matthew, Park Road East
OR C 1889-1969, M 1914-69, Banns 1914-27, B 1961-69 (CRO)

BIRKENHEAD St Winifred (Welsh Church), Westbourne Road b 1891

BIRKENHEAD St Mark, Devonshire Road created a parish in 1922 from St John the Evangelist
OR C 1894-1957, M 1895-1963 (CRO)
Cop (Mf) C 1894-1942, M 1895-1933 (CRO, Manchester Local Hist Lib)

BIRKENHEAD All Saints and St Bede, Shrewsbury Road (created a parish from Bidston and Oxton, 1911, united to St James, 1972)
OR C 1888-1947, M 1911-71, Banns 1911-68 (CRO)

BIRKENHEAD St Bede, Park Road West, Claughton mission church, 1888

BIRKENHEAD Brunswick Chapel, Price Street b 1830 (Wesleyan Methodist; Birkenhead Circuit) closed 1960
OR ZC 1830-37 (PRO: RG 4/305); C 1830-1958, M 1867-1954 (CRO)
Cop (Mf) ZC 1830-37 (CRO, SLC); C 1830-1916 (CRO)

BIRKENHEAD St Werburgh, Grange Road (Roman Catholic) f 1834

BIRKENHEAD Parkfield (Welsh Presbyterian) f 1837 (K 1924)

BIRKENHEAD The Woodlands, Hamilton Terrace (1839), later Price Street (1852) (Welsh Baptist) b 1889 (K 1946)

BIRKENHEAD St Andrew, Conway Street (Presbyterian) b 1840 (K 1924-46)

BIRKENHEAD Clifton Road (Welsh Independent) b 1844, reb 1881 (K 1946)
OR C 1842-54, B 1847 (National Library of Wales)

BIRKENHEAD St Paul, Regent Place, Grange Road (Presbyterian) f 1848, destroyed 1976

BIRKENHEAD Charing Cross later (1903) Bessborough Road, Oxton later (1960) **Clive Hall**, Clive Road f 1851 (Unitarian)
OR C 1888-1921 (CRO)

BIRKENHEAD Our Lady of the Immaculate Conception and St Edward the Confessor, Cavendish Street (Roman Catholic) f 1854

BIRKENHEAD Grange Road (Primitive Methodist: First Circuit) f 1855, b 1870, closed 1958
OR C 1886-1958, M 1916-58 (CRO)

BIRKENHEAD Oxton Road and Balls Road (Independent) b 1856, reb 1923, *fl.* 1987

BIRKENHEAD Palm Grove Chapel, Talbot Lane later Lorne Road (Wesleyan Methodist: Birkenhead Circuit) f 1858, b 1871, closed 1978
OR C 1858-80, 1887, M 1875-1977 (CRO)

BIRKENHEAD Grange Road Chapel, Grange Road (Baptist) b 1858, *fl.* 1989

BIRKENHEAD St Anne, Highfield Road, Rock Ferry (Roman Catholic) f 1862

BIRKENHEAD St Laurence, Beckwith Street (Roman Catholic) f 1864

BIRKENHEAD Claughton Road Chapel (United Methodist: St Domingo Circuit) b 1881, closed 1938
OR C 1864-1938, M 1927-38 (CRO)

BIRKENHEAD Lourd Street (Wesleyan Methodist) b 1864, destroyed 1941
OR C 1874-1941 (CRO)

BIRKENHEAD Hamilton Memorial Church, Upton Road (Presbyterian, later United Reformed Church) f 1868 b 1922, *fl.* 1991

BIRKENHEAD Grange Road (Wesleyan Methodist; Birkenhead Circuit) b 1872 (K 1946)

BIRKENHEAD Hind Street (Wesleyan Methodist; Birkenhead Circuit) b 1873, closed 1966
OR C 1873-1965, M 1965-66 (CRO)

BIRKENHEAD Lowe Street (Wesleyan Methodist; Birkenhead Circuit) b 1878, closed 1958
OR C 1879-1957 (CRO)

BIRKENHEAD Mount Tabor Chapel, Holt Road (Primitive Methodist) b 1879, closed 1966
OR C 1895-1945, M 1916-64 (CRO)

BIRKENHEAD Vittoria Street (Welsh Independent) f 1886 (K 1924)

BIRKENHEAD Holy Name of Jesus, Oxton (Roman Catholic) f 1899

BIRKENHEAD St Joseph, North Road (Roman Catholic) f 1900

BIRKENHEAD St John the Evangelist, Bebington Road, New Ferry (Roman Catholic) f 1902

BIRKENHEAD Laird Street Chapel, Laird Street (Baptist) f 1902, *fl.* 1989

BIRKENHEAD Laird Street (Welsh Presbyterian) f 1905 (K 1924)

BIRKENHEAD Woodchurch Road (Welsh Presbyterian) f 1906 (K 1924)

BIRKENHEAD Meeting House, Park Road South and Slater Street, Claughton (Society of Friends) f 1836 (K 1924). From 1831-1837 Birkenhead was in Lancashire Quarterly Meeting.
OR see Cheshire Quaker Registers; Lancashire Quaker Registers

BIRKENHEAD Church of Christ, Alvanley Place (Baptist) (K 1924)

BIRKENHEAD Beckwith Street (Primitive Methodist: First Circuit) (K 1924)

BIRKENHEAD Holy Cross, Hoylake Road (Roman Catholic) f 1928

BIRKINHEAD First Church of Christ, Scientist, Village Road, Oxton (Christian Science) (K 1946)

BIRKENHEAD St Michael and All Angels, Woodchurch (Roman Catholic) f 1952

BIRTLES St Catherine (54) chapel b 1840, township in Prestbury, created a parish in 1890 from Alderley and Prestbury
OR CMB 1890+ (Inc)

BIRTLES Over Alderley (United Methodist) b 1863 (K 1939)

BLACKDEN township in Sandbach (170)

BLACON cum CRABWALL township in Chester Holy Trinity (72)

BLACON Saughall Road (Independent, later United Reformed Church) f 1946

BLAKENHALL township in Wybunbury (245)

BOLLINFEE township in Wilmslow (1,784)

BOLLINGTON Holy Trinity (268) township part in Bowdon, part in Rostherne, created a parish in 1869
OR CMB 1870+ (Inc)
BT 1870-83 (+ index CB 1873-83) (CRO)

BOLLINGTON St John the Baptist (2,685) township in Prestbury, created a parish in 1842
OR C 1834-1958, M 1838-1959, B 1835-1937 (CRO)
BT 1841-78, 1888-93 (+ index CB 1873-78, 1888-93) (CRO)

BOLLINGTON Wellington Street (Wesleyan Methodist) f 1807 b 1886 (K 1939)
OR ZC 1812-36 (PRO: RG 4/573); B 1831-37 (PRO: RG 8/107); C 1841-1923 (CRO)

BOLLINGTON St Gregory, Chapel Street (Roman Catholic) b 1834 (K 1939)

BOLLINGTON High Street (Primitive Methodist) b 1859, closed 1956
OR C 1941-54, M 1901-52 (CRO)

BOLLINGTON Palmerston Street (Independent) b 1867 (K 1939)

BOLLINGTON Grimshaw Lane (United Methodist) b *c*1887, closed 1956
OR C 1889-1956 (CRO)

BOLLINGTON Kerridge (Wesleyan Methodist) b 1895, closed 1982

BOLLINGTON CROSS St Oswald chapel of ease to Prestbury
OR C 1908-64, M 1937-68 (CRO)

BOSDEN part of township of Handforth cum Bosden

BOSLEY St Mary (597) chapelry in Prestbury, created a parish in 1883
OR C 1728-1847, M 1729-50, Banns 1859-1987, B 1728-1847 (CRO); M 1859+ (Inc)
BT 1615, 1617, 1619-23, 1625-27, 1634-36, 1637?, 1639, 1641, 1662-81, 1695, 1700, 1718, 1720-26, 1728-1878, 1880-93 (+ index CB 1874-93) (CRO)
Cop M 1729-50 (Ptd, Phil 5, 1913); M 1729-50 (Boyd, CMI, NCMI)
Cop (Mf) C 1728-1847, M 1729-50, Banns 1859-1987, B 1728-1847 (CRO)

BOSLEY (Wesleyan Methodist) b 1832, reb 1885, *fl.*1942

BOSTOCK township in Davenham (218)

BOUGHTON, GREAT township in Chester St Oswald (900)

BOWDON Blessed Virgin Mary (8,200) [Bucklow Hundred; Altrincham Union]
OR C 1628-1841, M 1628-1844, Banns 1842-1961, B 1628-1841 (CRO)
BT 1600, 1606-07, 1610, 1614, 1618, 1621-22, 1626-29, 1631-33, 1635-37, 1640, 1660, 1663, 1666, 1668-76, 1678-85, 1689-92, 1694-1702, 1704-37, 1739-1843, 1845-1914 (+ index CB 1873-92) (CRO)
Cop M 1628-99 (Ts CRO); M 1814, 1830-37 (CMI)
Cop (Mf) C 1628-1841, M 1628-1844, B 1628-1841 (CRO, Manchester Local Hist Lib)

BRADLEY township in Malpas (95)

BRADWALL township in Sandbach (297)

BRAMHALL St Michael and All Angels (1,401) township in Stockport, created a parish in 1911
OR C 1891-1939, M 1903-40 (CRO))

BRAMHALL Woodford Road (Baptist) b 1856, *fl.*1989
OR Z 1866+ (Ch Sec)
Cop Z 1866-76, 1883-92, B 1860-1911 (SG)

BRAMHALL Christian Bethel (Free Gospel) b 1866

BRAMHALL Bramhall Lane (Wesleyan Methodist) b 1871 (K 1928)

BRAMHALL (Independent) b 1902 (K 1928)

BREDBURY St Mark (2,374) township in Stockport, created a parish in 1846
OR C 1847-88, M 1849-1992, Banns 1934-85, B 1848-1980 (CRO)
BT 1879-88, 1890-92 (+ index CB 1879-88, 1890-92) (CRO)

BREDBURY Hatherlow (Independent) f 1645, b 1706, reb 1846 (K 1939)

BREDBURY Woodley (Primitive Methodist) b 1868 (K 1939)

BREDBURY George Lane (Independent) b 1912 (K 1939)

BREDBURY Our Lady of St Christopher, Barrack Hill (Roman Catholic) f 1912, b 1932

BRERETON St Oswald (661) [Northwich Hundred; Congleton Union] (united to Swettenham, 1971)
OR C 1538-1850, M 1538-1860, B 1538-1869 (CRO)
BT 1593, 1595, 1606, 1613-15, 1617-20, 1623, 1625-26, 1630-35, 1658-66, 1668-76, 1679-82, 1684-85, 1691-1794, 1796-1840 (CRO)
Cop M 1754-1837 (SG, NCMI); M 1691-1836 (CMI)
Cop (Mf) C 1538-1850, M 1538-1860, B 1538-1869 (CRO, Manchester Local Hist Lib)

BRERETON (Calvinist Dissenters) (Lewis 1831)

BRERETON Davenport Chapel (Wesleyan Methodist) b 1835, *fl.*1967

BRERETON (Primitive Methodist) b 1882, closed *c*1923

BRIDGEMERE township in Wybunbury (236)

BRIGHTON, NEW St James created a parish in 1861 from Wallasey
OR C 1856-1920, M 1860-1934 (CRO)
Cop (Mf) C 1856-1911, M 1860-1908 (CRO)

BRIGHTON, NEW Emmanuel, Sea Bank Road, created a parish in 1909 from New Brighton St James
OR CM 1905+ (Inc)

BRIGHTON, NEW All Saints, Hose Side, b 1909, created a parish in 1929 from New Brighton St James and Wallasey
OR M 1929-83 (CRO); C 1929+ (Inc)

BRIGHTON, NEW Rake Lane (Welsh Presbyterian) f 1872 (K 1924)

BRIGHTON, NEW St Peter and St Paul, Atherton Street (Roman Catholic) f 1881

BRIGHTON, NEW Seabank Road (Baptist) f 1890, *fl.*1989

BRIGHTON, NEW St Andrew, Ennerdale Road, Warren Drive (Presbyterian, later United Reformed Church) f 1903, *fl.*1991

BRIMSTAGE township in Bromborough (136)

BRINDLEY township in Acton (153)

BRINNINGTON St Luke created a parish in 1963 from Portwood and Bredbury
OR CM 1963+ (Inc)

BROADBOTTOM St Mary created a parish in 1890
OR CM 1890+ (Inc)

BROADHEATH St Albert created a parish in 1911 from Altrincham
OR C 1899-1910, M 1911-68, Banns 1956-78 (CRO)

BROMBOROUGH St Barnabas (449) [Wirral Hundred; Wirral Union]
OR C 1580-1922, M 1580-1919, B 1580-1905 (CRO)
BT 1600, 1605, 1607-10, 1612, 1615-22, 1626-27, 1630, 1636, 1638, 1641-42, 1658-60, 1679-82, 1684-85, 1703-05, 1707-35, 1741, 1744, 1746-47, 1749-61, 1767-78, 1780-92, 1794, 1796, 1798-1801, 1805-37, 1840-49, 1851, 1855-1905 (+ index CB 1873-93) (CRO)
Cop 1600-1726 (Ptd, A. Anderson, 1962); M 1701-35, 1744-47, 1751-1837 (CMI)
Cop (Mf) C 1580-1922, M 1580-1919, B 1580-1905 (CRO, Wirral Archives, Manchester Local Hist Lib)

BROMBOROUGH (Wesleyan Methodist: Bebington Circuit) b 1928 (K 1946)

BROMBOROUGH Christ the King, New Chester Road (Roman Catholic) f 1928

BROMHALL township in Wrenbury (181)

BROXTON township in Malpas (454)

BRUERA St Mary township in Chester St Oswald, created a parish in 1868
OR C 1657-1949, M 1665-1837, B 1657-1899 (CRO)
BT 1666, 1668-77, 1679, 1681-85, 1689, 1691-92, 1694-1700, 1703-09, 1711, 1713-15, 1717-18, 1720-26, 1728-29, 1731, 1733-1756, 1759-63, 1765-1828, 1830, 1832-40, 1872-84 (+ index C 1873-83) (CRO)
Cop 1662-1812 (Ptd, W.F. Irvine, PRS 67, 1910); M 1665-1837 (Boyd); M 1662-1812 (NCMI); M 1665-1816 (CMI)

BUDWORTH, GREAT St Mary and All Saints (15,955) [part Bucklow Hundred, part Eddisbury Hundred; Runcorn Union]
OR C 1558-1984, M 1558-1989, Banns 1754-1885, 1950-89, B 1558-1892 (CRO)
BT 1605-07, 1612-14, 1616-23, 1625, 1627-28, 1630-31, 1634, 1637-41, 1658-62, 1665-67, 1669-71, 1673, 1675-76, 1677?, 1678-85, 1690-1738, 1741-1838, 1840-44, 1870-1907 (+ index CB 1873-93) (CRO)
Cop M 1700-1900 (MCMI); M 1690-98, 1825-28, 1834-37 (CMI)
Cop (Mf) C 1558-1872, M 1558-1912, B 1558-1892 (CRO, Northwich Lib, Manchester Local Hist Lib)

BUDWORTH, GREAT Allostock (Prot.Dissenters later Unitarian) f 1672, closed 1970s
OR ZCB 1779-1823 (PRO: RG 4/2259); ZC 1688-1755, M 1690-1701, B 1690-1755 (PRO: RG 8/4)
Cop ZC 1778-1823 (Ptd, W.R. Strachan, 1982); B 1827-72 (CRO)
Cop (Mf) ZCB 1779-1823 (CRO, SLC)

BUDWORTH, GREAT Pickmere (Wesleyan Methodist: Northwich Circuit) f 1770, b 1826, *fl.*1973
OR ZC 1811-39 (PRO: RG 4/2149)
Cop (Mf) ZC 1811-39 (CRO, SLC)

BUDWORTH, GREAT Comberbach (Wesleyan Methodist) b 1817, reb 1879, *fl.*1988

BUDWORTH, GREAT Plumley (Wesleyan Methodist) b 1827, reb 1887, *fl.*1954

BUDWORTH, GREAT Bradshaw Brook, Allostock (Wesleyan Methodist) b 1835, reb 1960

BUDWORTH, GREAT Bartington (Wesleyan Methodist) b *c*1840, *fl.*1973

BUDWORTH, GREAT Wincham (Wesleyan Methodist) b 1846, reb 1875, closed 1964
OR C 1869-1953, M 1913-57 (CRO)

BUDWORTH, GREAT Over Whitley (Society of Friends). From 1802 to 1837 Great Budworth was in Lancashire Quarterly Meeting.
OR see Cheshire Quaker Registers; Lancashire Quaker Registers
BT 1865-67 (CRO)

BUDWORTH, GREAT Winnington (Primitive Methodist) b 1898, *fl.*1968

BUDWORTH, GREAT Anderton (Primitive Methodist) b *c*1910, closed 1969
OR M 1916-55 (CRO)

BUDWORTH, LITTLE St Peter (621) [Eddisbury Hundred; Northwich Union]
OR C 1561-1921, M 1561-1837, Banns 1845-1945, B 1561-1875 (CRO)
BT 1576, 1585, 1604, 1607-09, 1613-15, 1617, 1625, 1629-30, 1633-37, 1639, 1658-61, 1663-65, 1669-76, 1679-85, 1688-1840, 1846-97 (+ index CB 1873-93) (CRO)
Cop M 1700-1900 (MCMI); M 1813-37 (NCMI); M 1680-1837 (CMI)
Cop (Mf) C 1561-1921, M 1561-1837, B 1561-1875 (CRO, Manchester Local Hist Lib)

BUDWORTH, LITTLE (Wesleyan Methodist) b 1888, *fl.*1924

BUERTON township in Aldford

BUERTON township in Audlem

BUGLAWTON St John the Evangelist (2,087) chapelry in Astbury, created a parish in 1841
OR C 1840-1957, M 1841-1950, B 1839-1939 (CRO)
BT 1893-94, 1928 (in Astbury BT from 1841) (+ index C 1893) (CRO)
Cop (Mf) C 1840-1895, M 1841-1891, B 1839-1939 (CRO, Manchester Local Hist Lib)

BUGLAWTON Key Green (Wesleyan Methodist) b 1821, reb 1845, *fl.*1984

BUGLAWTON Mill Street (Primitive Methodist) f 1823, *fl.*1965

BUGLAWTON Dane-in-Shaw (Wesleyan Methodist) b 1824, reb 1898, closed 1973
OR M 1911-56 (CRO)

BUGLAWTON Timbersbrook Chapel (Primitive Methodist) b 1883, closed 1969

BULKELEY township in Malpas

BUNBURY St Boniface (4,373) [part Eddisbury Hundred, part Broxton Hundred; Nantwich Union]
OR C 1598-1953, M 1559-1982, Banns 1754-1812, 1859-1900, B 1559-1922 (CRO)
BT 1588, 1593, 1600, 1605, 1608, 1610-11, 1614-18, 1620-24, 1626-33, 1636-39, 1641, 1658-68, 1670-74, 1676-77, 1679-85, 1687-92, 1694-99, 1701-16, 1718-19, 1721-22, 1725-42, 1744-54, 1757-1868 (CRO)
Cop C 1598-1773, M 1559-1740, B 1564-1828 (Chester AS); M 1701-16, 1757-67, 1813-37 (CMI)
Cop (Mf) C 1598-1953, M 1559-1876, B 1559-1922 (CRO, Manchester Local Hist Lib)

BUNBURY Trinity Chapel (Wesleyan Methodist) b 1806, reb 1868 (K 1939)
OR C 1839-81 in Tarporley Circuit register (CRO)

BUNBURY Grove Chapel, Alpraham (Wesleyan Methodist) b 1828, closed 1962
OR M 1931-62 (CRO)

BUNBURY Alpraham (Primitive Methodist) b 1844, reb 1882
OR M 1905-62 (CRO)

BUNBURY Radmore Green Chapel, Spurstow (Primitive Methodist) b 1841, reb 1905
OR M 1907-65 (CRO)

BUNBURY Tiverton Chapel (Primitive Methodist) b 1864, *fl.*1938

BUNBURY (Primitive Methodist) b 1876, closed 1970
OR M 1931-67 (CRO)

BUNBURY Beeston (Primitive Methodist) b 1911, closed 1971

BURLAND township in Acton (515)

BURLEYDAM St Michael created a parish in 1738 from Wrenbury
OR C 1770-1958, B 1869-73 (CRO)
BT 1869-79, 1883-86, 1915-22 (+ index CB 1873-86) (CRO)
Cop (Mf) C 1770-1958 (CRO)

BURTON St Nicholas (458) [Wirral Hundred; Wirral Union]
OR C 1538-1885, M 1538-1966, Banns 1844-1946, B 1538-1993 (CRO)
BT 1599-1603, 1606-10, 1613-14, 1617-19, 1621-25, 1629-30, 1632, 1634, 1636, 1638, 1642, 1658-60, 1666-76, 1679-85, 1690, 1695, 1722, 1724, 1763, 1779-98, 1800-30, 1855-1900 (+ index CB 1873-93) (CRO)
Cop 1538-1725 (Ptd, F.C. Beazley, *Transactions of the Historic Society of Lancashire and Cheshire* 59, NS 23, 1907); 1538-1770 (CRO); M 1756-66, 1779-97, 1800-35 (CMI)
Cop (Mf) C 1538-1885, M 1538-1835, B 1538-1897 (CRO, Wirral Archives, Manchester Local Hist Lib)

BURTON by TARVIN township in Tarvin (84)

BURTONWOOD St Michael ancient parish in Lancashire, transferred to Cheshire, 1974 *see* Lancashire NIPR

BURWARDSLEY St John (394) [part Broxton Hundred, part Eddisbury Hundred; Nantwich Union] created a parish in 1767 from Bunbury
OR C 1818-94, Banns 1885-1903, B 1822-1845 (CRO); M 1837+ (Inc)
BT 1818-47. 1851-55, 1877-84 (+ index CB 1877-82, 1884) (CRO)
Cop M 1739-48, 1750-59 (CMI)
Cop (Mf) C 1818-94 (CRO)

BURWARDSLEY (Primitive Methodist) b 1843 (K 1939)

BUTLEY township in Prestbury (808)

BYLEY cum LEES St John the Evangelist (123) township in Middlewich created a parish in 1848
OR C 1848-1906, Banns 1864-1968, B 1849-98 (CRO); M 1864+ (Inc)
BT 1855-60, 1881-93 (+ index CB 1881-91) (CRO)
Cop (Mf) C 1848-1906, Banns 1864-1968, B 1849-98 (CRO)

CADISHEAD St Mary created a parish in 1925 from Irlam and Flixton in Lancashire and Partington and Carrington in Cheshire
OR CM 1925+ (Inc)

CALDECOTT township in Shocklach (75)

CALDY township in West Kirby (102)
OR M 1933-80 (CRO)

CALVELEY township in Bunbury (170)

CAPENHURST Holy Trinity (159) township in Shotwick, created a parish in 1859
OR C 1859-1990, Banns 1860-1976 (CRO); MB 1857+ (Inc)
BT 1859-78, 1892 (+ index CB 1873-77) (CRO)

CAPENHURST Resurrection and All Saints
OR M 1933-80 (CRO); C 1907+ (Inc)

CAPENHURST Ledsham (Welsh Presbyterian) (K 1928)

CAPESTHORNE Holy Trinity (72) township and chapel in Prestbury, united to Siddington, 1846
OR C 1718-1895, M 1722-47, 1783-84, 1965, 1968, B 1724-1874 (CRO)
BT 1722-42, 1744-86, 1788-1846, 1849, 1856-57, 1859-63 (CRO)
Cop M 1722-47 (Ptd, Phil 5, 1913); M 1722-47 (Boyd, CMI, NCMI)
Cop (Mf) C 1718-1895, M 1722-47, 1783-84, 1965, 1968, B 1724-1874 (CRO)

CARDEN township in Tilston (249)

CARRINGTON St George chapelry in Bowdon, created a parish in 1759
OR C 1759-1889, B 1760-1894 (CRO); M 1844+ (Inc)
BT 1876-95 (+ index CB 1876-87) (CRO)
Cop (Mf) C 1759-1889, B 1760-1894 (CRO)

CASTLE HALL Holy Trinity (Stalybridge) created a parish in 1846 from Stockport
OR C 1852-89, M 1852-92, B 1853-79 (CRO)
BT 1892 (CRO)

CAUGHALL township in Backford

CHADKIRK St Chad alias ROMILEY (1,290) created a parish in 1745 from Stockport
OR C 1748-1910, M 1748-1754, B 1748-1868 (CRO)
BT 1790-1817, 1867-1913 (+ index CB 1873-91) (CRO)
Cop M 1748-54 (CMI)
Cop (Mf) C 1748-1889, M 1748-1754, B 1748-1868 (CRO)

CHADKIRK Romiley (Wesleyan Methodist) (K 1928)

CHADKIRK Romiley (Primitive Methodist) (K 1928)

CHEADLE St Mary the Virgin (4,119) [Macclesfield Hundred; Stockport Union]
OR C 1558-1880, M 1558-1913, B 1558-1911 (CRO)
BT 1610, 1619, 1625, 1630, 1633, 1635-41, 1663-85, 1690, 1695, 1727, 1730-35, 1737-38, 1744-46, 1748-1852, 1873-86, 1888 (+ index CB 1873-86, 1888) (CRO)
Cop M 1558-1837 (NCMI); M 1662-1714, 1741-1801 (CMI)
Cop (Mf) C 1677-1713, M 1662-1796, B 1677-78 (SG)

CHEADLE All Hallows chapel of ease to Cheadle St Mary the Virgin
OR CM 1969+ (Inc)

CHEADLE Bullock Smithy alias Hazel Grove (Wesleyan Methodist) f 1788
OR ZC 1794-1837, B 1819-37 (PRO: RG 4/159)
Cop (Mf) ZC 1794-1837, B 1819-37 (CRO, SLC)

CHEADLE Edgeley (Wesleyan Methodist) f 1817
OR B 1818-37 (PRO: RG 4/536-537)
Cop (Mf) B 1818-37 (CRO, SLC)

CHEADLE St John (Methodist New Connexion) (Lewis 1831) reb 1883

CHEADLE Zion Chapel, Stretford Road, Hulme (Independent) (Lewis 1831) reb 1861
OR C 1824-43 (Manchester Local Hist Lib)

CHEADLE (Primitive Methodist) b 1835, *fl.* 1892

CHEADLE Swan Lane, Cheadle Hulme (Independent) b 1869

CHEADLE St Chad, Stockport Road (Roman Catholic) f 1900

CHEADLE St Ann, Vicarage Avenue, Cheadle Hulme (Roman Catholic) b 1952

CHEADLE Christ Church, Finney Lane, Heald Green (Roman Catholic) f 1959

CHEADLE Sacred Heart, Stockport Road, Cheadle Heath (Roman Catholic) f 1962

CHEADLE BULKELEY township in Cheadle

CHEADLE HULME All Saints created a parish in 1868 from Cheadle and Gatley
OR M 1869-1935 (CRO); C 1863+ (Inc)

CHEADLE HULME St Andrew created a parish in 1868 from Cheadle and Gatley
OR CM 1959+ (Inc)

CHEADLE MOSELEY township in Cheadle

CHECKLEY cum WRINEHILL township in Wybunbury (235)

CHELFORD St John the Evangelist (191) chapelry in Prestbury, created a parish in 1720
[Macclesfield Hundred; Macclesfield Union]
OR C 1679-1849, M 1674-1752, B 1675-1894 (CRO)
BT 1839-1902 (in Prestbury BT to 1838) (+ index CB 1873-78) (CRO)
Cop M 1674-1752 (Ptd, Phil 5, 1913); M 1674-1752 (Boyd, NCMI); M 1729-46 (CMI)
Cop (Mf) C 1679-1849, B 1675-1894 (CRO, Manchester Local Hist Lib);
C 1777-94, B 1748-76 (SG)

CHELFORD Snelson (Wesleyan Methodist) b 1825 (K 1928)

CHESHIRE QUAKER REGISTERS (Society of Friends)
OR (Cheshire Quarterly Meeting) Z 1648-1783, M 1667-1765, B 1655-1782
(PRO: RG 6/1031, 1035, 1037, 1256); (Cheshire and Staffordshire Quarterly Meeting) Z 1783-1836, M 1768-1837, B 1783-1837 (PRO: RG 6/180, 285-288, 294, 297, 303); (Morley Monthly Meeting later Cheshire Monthly Meeting) Z 1654-1830, M 1654-1831, B 1654-1776 (PRO: RG 6/96, 157, 181, 213, 1036, 1398); (Monthly Meeting of Cheshire) Z 1776-99, 1833-37, M 1831-37, B 1831-37 (PRO: RG 6/256)
Cop Z 1648-1836, M 1667-1837, B 1655-1837 (CRO, SLC); M 1754-1837 (NCMI)

CHESTER Board of Guardians
OR Z 1914-43, B 1882-1900 (Chester RO)

CHESTER Castle extra-parochial area (32)

CHESTER Cemetery, Overleigh Road (13 acres) opened 1850
OR B 1850+ (Cemetery)
Cop (Mf) B 1850-1990 (Chester RO)

CHESTER Spittle-Boughton extra-parochial area (131)

CHESTER St John the Baptist, Vicars Lane (6,035)
OR C 1559-1940, M 1559-1956, Banns 1754-1812, B 1559-1915 (CRO)
BT 1599-1601, 1604-05, 1610-11, 1612?, 1613-15, 1617-18, 1622-25, 1627-31, 1633-35, 1662-63, 1666, 1668-77, 1679-84, 1686-91, 1693-1728, 1731, 1733-1839, 1875-1878 (+ index C 1875-78) (CRO)
Cop C 1559-1779, M 1559-1734, 1754-93, B 1559-1754 (CRO); 1622-70, 1717-23 (Chester AS); C 1790-91 (Ts CRO, SG); M 1735-40 (SG); M 1790 (CMI)
Cop (Mf) C 1559-1940, M 1559-1956, B 1559-1915 (CRO, Manchester Local Hist Lib)

CHESTER St Bridget united to St Martin 1842 (747)
OR C 1649-1972, M 1649-1972, Banns 1868-1903, 1961-72, B 1649-1896 (CRO)
BT 1600-01, 1603-04, 1611-13, 1615-17, 1622, 1624-25, 1627-32, 1634, 1637, 1639-42, 1663, 1666, 1668-85, 1691-1728, 1730-34, 1737-80, 1782-90, 1792-1802, 1804-27, 1829-56, 1858-94, 1896 (+ index CB 1873-91) (CRO)
Cop 1560-1642 (British Lib: Harleian Ms 2177; SG, Ptd in *Cheshire Sheaf* 3rd series 15-18, 1920-23); C 1818-32 (Ptd, *Family History Society of Cheshire Journal*, 3 (1), 1972); C 1813-32 (SG); M 1560-1642 (NCMI); M 1710-18, 1756-1837 (CMI)
Cop (Mf) C 1649-1972, M 1649-1972, B 1649-1896 (CRO, Manchester Local Hist Lib)

CHESTER St Oswald, Parkgate Street (6,041)
OR C 1581-1945, M 1581-1969, Banns 1754-1812, B 1581-1854 (CRO)
BT 1603-05, 1608-10, 1613-14, 1616-18, 1622-25, 1629, 1636-41, 1666-67, 1669-77, 1679-85, 1690, 1693-1716, 1718-31, 1733-81, 1783-1838 (CRO)
Cop M 1581-1700 (Ptd, *Cheshire Sheaf* 3rd series, 2-3, 1898-1901; 1580-1797 (Chester AS); M 1581-1700 (CRO, SG, NCMI); CB 1581-1628 (SG); M 1801-13, 1833-37 (CMI)
Cop (Mf) C 1581-1945, M 1581-1969, B 1581-1854 (CRO, Manchester Local Hist Lib)

CHESTER St Michael, Bridge Street united to St Olave, 1839
OR C 1581-1970, M 1581-1972, Banns 1754-1812, 1823-1972, B 1581-1848 (CRO)
BT 1600-01, 1604, 1611, 1613-14, 1622, 1624, 1627-35, 1637, 1639-42, 1661-63, 1666-77, 1679-85, 1690-91, 1693-1743, 1746-1816, 1828-39, 1868, 1876 (+ index C 1876) (CRO)
Cop CB 1581-1851, M 1581-1812 (Chester AS); M 1747-1836 (CMI)
Cop (Mf) C 1581-1970, M 1581-1972, B 1581-1848 (CRO, Manchester Local Hist Lib)

CHESTER St Peter, The Cross (863)
OR C 1588-1956, M 1588-1970, Banns 1754-89, 1823-1904, B 1588-1846 (CRO)
BT 1600, 1604, 1610-11, 1613-15, 1617, 1625-27, 1629-35, 1637-40, 1663, 1666-76, 1679-80, 1682, 1684, 1700, 1710-11, 1714-17, 1719-20, 1723-25, 1727, 1732-39, 1742-44, 1746, 1748-49, 1751-67, 1769-1843, 1845-79 (+ index C 1873-79) (CRO)
Cop M 1754-1837 (CMI)
Cop (Mf) C 1588-1956, M 1588-1913, B 1588-1846 (CRO, Manchester Local Hist Lib)

CHESTER Holy Trinity, Watergate Street (3,298)
OR 1598-1653 (British Lib: Harleian Ms 2177); C 1656-1925, M 1654-1939, B 1656-1854 (CRO)
BT 1599-1601, 1604, 1610-11, 1614-18, 1622-23, 1625-35, 1639, 1641, 1663, 1666-77, 1679-85, 1690, 1695-96, 1700-11, 1713-21,1723-51,1753-54,1756-1813, 1815-29, 1834, 1836-93 (+ index C 1873-91) (CRO)
Cop CM 1598-1837, B 1532-1837 (early B taken from churchwarden's accounts, etc.) (Ptd, L.M. Farrall, 1914); 1654-1812 (Chester AS); M 1598-1837 (NCMI); M 1742-73, 1794-1834 (CMI)
Cop (Mf) C 1656-1828, M 1654-1834, B 1656-1854 (CRO, Manchester Local Hist Lib)

CHESTER St Olave united to St Michael, 1839 (456)
OR C 1611-1861, M 1611-1861, Banns 1754-1811, 1823-59, B 1611-1849 (CRO)
BT 1599-1601, 1604, 1610, 1614, 1617, 1622, 1624-25, 1629-30, 1632, 1638-40, 1668-77, 1679-85, 1690-91, 1693-1846 (1627-28, 1631, 1633-35, 1637, 1641-42 in Chester St Michael BT) (CRO)
Cop 1611-73 (British Lib: Harleian Ms 2177, SG); M 1701-38, 1756-1837 (CMI)
Cop (Mf) C 1611-1861, M 1611-1861, B 1611-1849 (CRO, Manchester Local Hist Lib)

CHESTER St Mary on the Hill or St Mary within the Walls, St Mary's Hill (3,545)
OR C 1628-1949, M 1628-1975, Banns 1754-72, B 1628-1854 (CRO)
BT 1601, 1604-05, 1616, 1622, 1624-25, 1627, 1630, 1663, 1666-75, 1677, 1679-86, 1688-1795, 1798, 1800, 1802-04, 1806-07, 1809-94 (+ index C 1873-92) (CRO)
Cop 1547-1812 (Ptd, *The history of the church and parish of St Mary-on-the-Hill, Chester*, J.P. Earwaker and R.H. Morris, 1898); C 1547-53, 1570-72, M 1548-51, B 1547-53 (British Lib: Harleian Ms 2177, CRO); CMB 1601-28 (BT) (CRO); 1547-1628 (Ptd, *Cheshire Sheaf*, 4th Series 2, 1967); C 1600-1700 (Ptd, *Family History Society of Cheshire Journal* 7-9, 1977-80); B 1837-42 (Ptd, *Family History Society of Cheshire Journal* 2-4, 1971-72); C 1820-24 (Ptd, *Family History Society of Cheshire Journal* 2, 1971)
Cop (Mf) C 1628-1898, M 1628-1910, B 1628-1854 (CRO, Manchester Local Hist Lib); C 1628-46, 1813-14, 1820-31 (SG)

CHESTER St Martin, St Martin's Ash (Welsh Church) (528) united to St Bridget, 1842
OR C 1671-1963, M 1671-1842, B 1671-1842 (CRO)
BT 1600-01, 1602?, 1611-12, 1614, 1617, 1622, 1627-32, 1635, 1638-40, 1666, 1670-73, 1675, 1677, 1679-85, 1688-91, 1693-1739, 1741-42, 1744, 1746-61, 1763-66, 1768-76, 1780-1842 (1624-25 in Chester St Mary BT) (CRO)
Cop 1680-1791 (Chester AS); M 1701-20, 1763-76, 1791-1838 (CMI)
Cop (Mf) C 1671-1963, M 1671-1842, B 1671-1842 (CRO, Manchester Local Hist Lib)

CHESTER St Werburgh, later Christ and the Blessed Virgin Mary (Chester Cathedral)
OR C 1688-1718, 1736-1958, M 1688-1718, 1736-1981, Banns 1870-1940, B 1688-1721, 1736-1896 (CRO)
BT 1813-16 (CRO)
Cop 1687-1812 (Ptd, T. Hughes, PRS 54, 1904); M 1735-54 (NCMI); M 1687-1718, 1735-54 (CMI)
Cop (Mf) C 1688-1935, M 1688-1851, B 1813-96 (CRO)

CHESTER Christ Church, off St Anne Street (created from St Oswald and Hoole, 1843)
OR C 1838-1955, M 1871-1972, B 1839-54 (CRO)
BT 1855, 1857-76 (+ index C 1873-76) (CRO)

CHESTER St Paul, Boughton-in-the-City created a parish in 1846 from St John the Baptist and St Oswald
OR C 1838-1919, M 1874-1934 (CRO)
BT 1838-70 (CRO)
Cop (Mf) C 1838-1919, M 1874-1934 (CRO, Manchester Local Hist Lib)

CHESTER St Barnabas
OR C 1877-1983 (CRO)

CHESTER Little St John extra-parochial place, united to St Oswald, 1867
OR C 1928-48 (CRO)

CHESTER Matthew Henry Memorial Church, Crook Street and Trinity Street or Newgate Street (Presbyterian, later United Reformed Church) f 1662 Presbyterian, Baptist *c*1706-68, then Unitarian, reb 1846, 1884, demolished 1960s
OR ZC 1713-1837, 1843-57, B 1791-1855 (PRO: RG 4/161, 2090, 3755)
Cop (Mf) ZC 1713-1837, 1843-57, B 1791-1855 (CRO, SLC)

CHESTER Meeting House, Frodsham Street (Society of Friends) b 1702, reb 1975
OR see Cheshire Quaker Registers

CHESTER Queens Street Chapel, later St Werburgh, Grosvenor Park Road (Roman Catholic) f 1757 b 1875 (K 1928)
OR ZC 1794-1956, M 1822-1973, DB 1861-1993 (CRO)

CHESTER Oldfield Drive, Vicar's Cross (Independent, later United Reformed Church) f 1772, *fl.* 1991
OR with Ch Sec

CHESTER Queen Street (Independent) b 1772, closed 1964
OR ZC 1803-37 (PRO: RG 4/160); C 1848-55, 1861-88, 1909-10, M 1848-55, 1880-88, B 1848-61, 1880 (Chester RO)
Cop (Mf) ZC 1803-37 (CRO, SLC)

CHESTER Commonhall Street (Baptist) f 1777, moved to Hamilton Place *c.* 1806

CHESTER St John Street (Wesleyan Methodist: Chester Circuit) b 1811 (K 1928)
OR ZC 1798-1837 (PRO: RG 4/162); C 1867-68 (Circuit) (in Tarporley Circuit register) (CRO)

CHESTER Octagon Chapel, Foregate Street (Calvinist Methodist)
OR ZCB 1805-06, 1817-35 (PRO: RG 4/70)
Cop (Mf) ZCB 1805-06, 1817-35 (CRO, SLC)

CHESTER Mount Zion Chapel, Common Hall Street (Calvinist Methodist) f 1820
OR ZC 1805-37 (PRO: RG 4/4417)
Cop (Mf) ZC 1805-37 (CRO, SLC)

CHESTER Pepper Street b *c.* 1833, moved to Grosvenor Park, 1880

CHESTER Steam Mill Street (Primitive Methodist Society)
OR ZC 1825-37 (PRO: RG 4/575); C 1845-1959 (Chester RO)
Cop (Mf) ZC 1825-37 (CRO, SLC)

CHESTER St Andrew, Newgate Street (United Reformed Church) f 1846, *fl.* 1991
OR Membership list 1878-1966 (Chester RO)

CHESTER Albion Park Welsh Chapel, Albion Street (Independent) b 1847 (K 1928)

CHESTER St Francis of Assissi, Grosvenor Street (Roman Catholic) f 1858
OR ZC 1859-1943, M 1865-1921, B 1860-1913 (CRO)

CHESTER Church Street, Upper Northgate Street (Catholic Apostolic) b 1864

CHESTER City Road (English Presbyterian) b 1864 (K 1928)

CHESTER St John Street (Welsh Calvinistic Methodist) b 1866 (K 1928)

CHESTER Great Boughton Chapel, Christleton Road (Independent, later United Reformed Church) b 1867, closed 1976
OR C 1872-1902, M 1874-78 (Chester RO)

CHESTER Central Hall, City Road (Wesleyan Methodist) b 1873, closed 1982
OR C 1873-1982, M 1900-82 (Chester RO)

CHESTER St Francis, Grosvenor Street (Roman Catholic) b 1875 (K 1928)

CHESTER Upper Northgate Street (Independent) b 1878, closed 1967

CHESTER Handbridge Chapel (Independent, later United Reformed Church) f 1876 b 1879, *fl.* 1991

CHESTER Grosvenor Park Road (Baptist) b 1880, closed late 1970s

CHESTER Ebenezer Mission Church, Milton Street b 1882 (K 1928)

CHESTER Welsh Wesleyan Chapel, Queen Street b 1884, closed *c*1972
OR M 1900-72 (Chester RO)

CHESTER Tarvin Road (Primitive Methodist: Chester Third Circuit) b 1884 (K 1928)
OR M 1921-83 (Chester RO)

CHESTER George Street (Primitive Methodist: Chester First Circuit) f 1863, b 1887, closed 1970
OR M 1917-69 (Chester RO)

CHESTER City Temple, Hunter Street (Primitive Methodist: Chester Second Circuit) b 1899, closed 1967
OR M 1916-67 (Chester RO)

CHESTER Sealand Road (Independent, later United Reformed Church) f 1909, *fl.*1991

CHESTER Pepper Street (United Methodist) closed *c*1920

CHESTER First Church of Christ Scientist, Pepper Street (K 1928)

CHESTER Gorse Stacks (Welsh Baptist) (K 1928)

CHESTER Church of Christ, Upper Northgate Street (K 1928)

CHESTER St John Street (Welsh Methodist) (K 1928)

CHESTER New Jerusalem Church, Victoria Road (Swedenborgian) (K 1928)

CHESTER Egerton Street (United Methodist) f 1920, closed 1932
OR C 1922-24 (Chester RO)

CHESTER Christadelphian Meeting Place, Queen Street (K 1928)

CHESTER Spiritualist Church, Brook Street (K 1928)

CHESTER Delamere Street (Plymouth Brethren) (K 1928)

CHESTER St Theresa, Blacon Avenue, Blacon (Roman Catholic) f 1956

CHIDLOW township in Malpas

CHILDER THORNTON *see* **THORNTON, CHILDER**

CHOLMONDELEY CHAPEL (272) township in Malpas
OR CMB 1840+ (Inc)
BT 1601, 1604, 1607-08, 1610, 1618, 1626-31, 1841-68 (CRO)

CHOLMONDESTON township in Acton (180)

CHORLEY St Philip renamed ALDERLEY EDGE (1894), Alderley Edge (474) township in in Wilmslow created a parish in 1855
OR C 1853-1924, M 1866-1959, Banns 1866-92, 1923-48 (CRO)
BT C 1853-1900 (+ index C 1873-93) (CRO)
Cop (Mf) C 1853-1924, M 1866-1914 (CRO)

CHORLEY Lindow (Methodist) b 1839, closed 1970
OR C 1891-1962 (CRO)

CHORLEY Alderley Edge (Methodist) b 1863
OR C 1863-1979 (CRO)

CHORLEY Brook Lane, Alderley Edge (United Baptist) b 1890

CHORLEY St Pius X, Stamford Road, Alderley Edge (Roman Catholic) b 1946

CHORLEY township in Wrenbury cum Frith (168)

CHORLTON township in Malpas (155)

CHORLTON township in Wybunbury (109)

CHORLTON by BACKFORD township in Backford (86)

CHOWLEY township in Coddington (70)

CHRISTLETON St James the Apostle (893) [Broxton Hundred; Great Boughton Union 1837-71, Chester Union 1871-1930]
OR C 1697-1954, M 1697-1970, Banns 1754-1812, 1883-1923, B 1697-1969 (CRO)
BT 1600-01, 1603-05, 1607-08, 1610-13, 1616, 1618, 1622-23, 1625, 1627, 1630-31, 1633,1635,1637,1640,1666-85,1690-92,1694-1707,1709-11,1713-1854,1859 (CRO)
Cop M 1697-1812 (Ptd, Phil 1, 1909); M 1701-1812 (Boyd); CMB 1600-1700 (BT) (Ptd, *Cheshire Sheaf* 3rd series 34-35, 1941-48); M 1600-97 (SG); M 1600-1812 (NCMI); M 1735-1837 (CMI)
Cop (Mf) C 1697-1954, M 1697-1970, B 1697-1969 (CRO, Manchester Local Hist Lib)

CHRISTLETON Milton Green (Methodist) b 1862, closed 1967
OR C 1916-74, M 1909-54 (Chester RO)

CHRISTLETON (Wesleyan Methodist) (Lewis 1831) b 1888 (K 1928)

CHRISTLETON Rowton (Wesleyan Methodist) b 1865 (K 1928)

CHURCH HULME see **HULME, CHURCH**

CHURCH LAWTON see **LAWTON, CHURCH**

CHURCH MINSHULL see **MINSHULL, CHURCH**

CHURTON by ALDFORD township in Aldford (238)

CHURTON by FARNDON township in Farndon (122)

CHURTON HEATH St Mary the Virgin *see* **BRUERA St Mary**

CHURTON HEATH Saighton (Presbyterian) b 1857 (K 1928)

CLAUGHTON Christ Church (224) b 1849, created a parish in 1876 from Bidston, Birkenhead St James and Oxton
OR C 1854-1963, M 1854-1961 (CRO)

CLAUGHTON cum GRANGE St Michael created a parish in 1912 from Claughton Christ Church and Tranmere
OR C 1898-1958, M 1898-1958 (CRO)

CLAUGHTON Trinity Church, Beresford Road (Presbyterian) f 1863 b 1866 (K 1946)

CLAVERTON extra-parochial place [Broxton Hundred; Hawarden Union]

CLIFTON township in Runcorn (36)

CLIVE township in Middlewich (123)

CLOTTON HOOFIELD township in Tarvin (401)

CLUTTON township in Farndon (100)

CODDINGTON St Mary (345) [Broxton Hundred; Great Boughton Union 1837-71, Tarvin Union 1871-1930]
OR C 1680-1718, 1820-1992, M 1680-1718, 1821-1982, B 1680-1718, 1820-1992 (CRO)
BT 1585, 1599, 1601, 1605-07, 1610, 1614, 1617-18, 1622-27, 1629-31, 1635, 1668-72, 1674-77, 1679-82, 1684-90, 1694, 1696, 1699, 1703, 1709, 1711-19, 1721, 1723-34, 1736-37, 1741-43, 1745-46, 1749, 1751-57, 1759-88, 1790-1833, 1840-45, 1854-1903 (+ index CB 1873-92) (CRO)
Cop 1599-1717 (BT) (CRO); 1680-1718 (Ts Index, CRO); M 1694-1719, 1751-88, 1792-1803, 1805-33 (CMI)

COGSHALL township in Great Budworth (77)

COMBERBACH township in Great Budworth (295)

COMPSTALL alias WERNETH St Paul township in Stockport created a parish in 1841
OR C 1839-65, B 1841-87 (CRO); M 1841+ (Inc)
BT 1847-54 (Lancs RO)

COMPSTALL (Wesleyan Methodist) f 1826 (K 1928)
OR ZC 1826-37 (PRO: RG 4/163)
Cop (Mf) ZC 1826-37 (CRO, SLC)

COMPSTALL (Unitarian) (Lewis 1831)

COMPSTALL (Primitive Methodist) (K 1928)

CONGLETON Board of Guardians
OR Z 1914-49, C 1902-51, D 1837-1963 (Chester RO)

CONGLETON St Peter's Cemetery (opened 1842: 1 acre; 1894: 2 acres; 1912: 4 acres)

CONGLETON St Peter (1,352) chapelry and borough in Astbury created a parish in 1720
OR C 1719-1917, M 1719-72, 1839-1931, B 1719-1913 (CRO)
BT 1745, 1749-50, 1752-86, 1789, 1792, 1796 (in Astbury BT 1787-88, 1790-91, 1793-95 and 1797-1898) (CRO)
Cop M 1711-54 (NCMI)
Cop (Mf) C 1719-1917, M 1719-72, 1839-1931, B 1719-1913 (CRO, Congleton Lib, Manchester Local Hist Lib); C 1750-69 (SG)

CONGLETON St James created from Congleton St Peter. 1844
OR C 1844-1925, M 1849-1947 (CRO)
BT 1886-94, 1904-14 (+ index CB 1886-91) (CRO)
Cop (Mf) C 1844-1901, M 1849-1908 (CRO)

CONGLETON St Stephen created a parish in 1845 from Congleton St Peter
OR C 1844-1962, M 1860-1958, Banns 1956-67, B 1860-1932 (CRO)

CONGLETON Cross Street (Unitarian) f 1662 reb 1883, closed 1978
OR C 1814-33 (PRO: RG 4/211); C 1936-74, M 1940-74, D 1934-77 (CRO)
Cop (Mf) C 1814-33 (CRO, SLC)

CONGLETON Meeting House (Society of Friends) closed *c*1741
OR B 1668-1831 (PRO: RG 6/97-98, 214, 1329); see also Cheshire Quaker Registers
Cop B 1668-1831 (CRO, SLC)

CONGLETON Wagg Street, Astbury (Wesleyan Methodist) f 1766, b 1808, reb as **Trinity Methodist Church**, 1967
OR ZC 1809-37 (PRO: RG 4/535); C 1838-98, M 1845-56 (CRO)
Cop (Mf) ZC 1809-37 (CRO, SLC)

CONGLETON Mill Street (1790), later (1876) Antrobus Street (Independent, later United Reformed Church) *fl.*1991
OR ZC 1785-1837 (PRO: RG 4/178); C 1785-1837, B 1834-37 (Manchester Local Hist Lib)
Cop (Mf) ZC 1785-1837 (CRO, SLC)

CONGLETON Lawton Street later (1888) Kinsey Street (Primitive Methodist) b 1821 (K 1928)

CONGLETON St Mary, West Road (Roman Catholic) f 1821 b 1826 (K 1928)

CONGLETON Zion Chapel (Lady Huntingdon's Connexion) f 1822
OR ZC 1822-37 (PRO: RG 4/173)
Cop (Mf) ZC 1822-37 (CRO, SLC)

CONGLETON Congleton Edge Chapel (Wesleyan Methodist) b 1833, reb 1889

CONGLETON Brook Street (Wesleyan Methodist) b 1834, closed 1966
OR C 1929-66 (CRO)

CONGLETON Queen Street (United Methodist: Burslem (Bethel) Circuit) b 1836 (K 1928)

CONGLETON Biddulph Road, Dane in Shaw (Primitive Methodist) b 1840 (K 1928)

CONGLETON Rood Lane (Wesleyan Methodist) f 1861, b 1886 (K 1928)

COOLE PILATE township in Acton (48)

COPPENHALL St Michael (498) [Nantwich Hundred; Nantwich Union]
OR C 1653-1935, M 1653-1934, B 1653-1857, Funerals 1938-55 (CRO)
BT 1579, 1593, 1599-1600, 1605, 1607-10, 1612-18, 1620-23, 1626, 1628-30, 1636-39, 1641, 1663, 1665-81, 1687, 1689, 1693, 1695-97, 1699-1704, 1708-57, 1759-88, 1791-1837, 1839, 1843-44, 1846-47, 1850-57, 1887-1907 (CRO)
Cop M 1754-1837 (NCMI); M 1653-68, 1694-1704, 1752-1837 (CMI)
Cop (Mf) C 1653-1869, M 1653-1895, B 1653-1857 (CRO, Manchester Local Hist Lib)

COPPENHALL (Primitive Methodist) b 1868, reb 1927 (K 1928)

COTEBROOK St John and Holy Cross b 1874 (chapel of ease to Tarporley)
OR M 1935-74 (CRO); CB 1875+ (Inc)

COTTON township in Sandbach (86)

COTTON ABBOTTS township in Christleton (11)

COTTON EDMUNDS township in Christleton (79)

CRANAGE township in Sandbach (438)

CREWE Christ Church, Moss Square (295) township in Barthomley, created a parish in 1855 from Coppenhall
OR C 1846-1910, M 1855-1912, B 1846-1912 (CRO)

CREWE St Paul
OR C 1869-1901, M 1870-1903 (CRO)

CREWE St Barnabas, West Street created a parish in 1886 from Coppenhall St Paul
OR CMB 1885+ (Inc)
BT C 1885-93 (+ index C 1885-93) (CRO)

CREWE St Peter, Earle Street created a parish in 1931 from Coppenhall St Paul and Coppenhall St Michael
OR CM 1894+ (Inc)

CREWE St John the Baptist created a parish in 1914 from Crewe Christ Church and Coppenhall St Paul
OR C 1914-66, M 1914-66, Banns 1914-51, 1965-71 (CRO)

CREWE St Andrew, Bedford Street created a parish in 1926 from Crewe Christ Church, Wistaston and Wybunbury
OR CM 1926+ (Inc)

CREWE All Saints, Wistaston Road
OR CM 1965+ (Inc)

CREWE Earle Street, later Market Terrace, Hightown (United Methodist) b 1843, reb 1883, *fl.*1956
OR C 1871-1903 (CRO)

CREWE St Mary of the Immaculate Conception, Gatefield and Delamere Street (Roman Catholic) f 1844 b 1890 (K 1928)
OR ZC 1856-1957, M 1857-1971, Banns 1924-28, DB 1856-1941, 1963-82 (CRO)

CREWE Oak Street later (1870) High Town (Independent) f 1847, *fl.*1972

CREWE Trinity Chapel, Mill Street (Wesleyan Methodist) f 1848, b 1877, closed 1967
OR C 1860-1967, M 1899-1966 (CRO)

CREWE Wedgwood Chapel, Heath Street (Primitive Methodist: Crewe First Circuit) b 1855, closed 1969
OR C 1850-1943, M 1906-69 (CRO)

CREWE Hill Street (Presbyterian) f 1862 (K 1928)

CREWE Wesley Street later (1865) Mill Street (Primitive Methodist: Crewe Second Circuit) f 1863, closed 1963
OR C 1864-99, M 1912-63 (CRO)

CREWE Sydney Chapel, Herbert Street (Primitive Methodist: Crewe First Circuit) b 1864, closed 1970
OR M 1933-62 (CRO)

CREWE Beech Street (Unitarian) b 1864, closed 1973

CREWE Ramsbottom Street (Primitive Methodist: Crewe First Circuit) f 1866, b 1875, closed 1969
OR M 1918-69 (CRO)

CREWE High Town (Wesleyan Methodist) b 1868, closed 1944
OR C 1867-1944, M 1899-1943 (CRO)

CREWE Warmingham Road (Wesleyan Methodist) b 1868, closed 1971
OR M 1928-66 (CRO)

CREWE Remer Street later (1869) North Street (Wesleyan Methodist)
OR C 1880-1951 (CRO)

CREWE Henry Street (Primitive Methodist: Crewe First Circuit) b 1880, closed *c*1976

CREWE Earle Street (Wesleyan Methodist) b 1881, closed 1948
OR C 1875-1947, M 1899-1947 (CRO)

CREWE Edleston Road (United Methodist) b 1881, closed 1934 and sold to Christian Scientists
OR C 1888-1934 (CRO)

CREWE Union Street (Baptist) f 1883, *fl.*1989

CREWE West Street, Oxford Street (Wesleyan Methodist) b 1887, closed 1958
OR C 1888-1951 (CRO)

CREWE Bradfield Road (Primitive Methodist: Crewe First Circuit) b 1899 to replace Leighton Moss Chapel (K 1928)

CREWE Ruskin Road (Primitive Methodist) b 1904, *fl.*1965

CREWE Minshull New Road (Primitive Methodist: Crewe First Circuit) b 1905, *fl.*1952

CREWE Flag Lane (Independent Methodist) *fl.*1914-62

CREWE Market Terrace (Salvation Army) (K 1928)

CREWE Baptist Tabernacle, West Street (K 1928)

CREWE Free Christian Church, Beech Street (K 1928)

CREWE Welsh Tabernacle, Derrington Street (K 1928)

CREWE GREEN St Michael created a parish in 1857 from Barthomley
OR CMB 1858+ (Inc)

CROFT with SOUTHWORTH Christ Church chapelry in Lancashire, transferred to Cheshire, 1974 *see* Lancashire NIPR

CROUGHTON township in Chester St Oswald (39)

CROWLEY township in Great Budworth (133)

CROWTON Christ Church (361) township in Weaverham created a parish in 1872 from Weaverham and Norley
OR C 1871-1948, M 1872-1977, B 1872-1972 (CRO)
BT 1871-98, 1900-01 (+ index CB 1873-90) (CRO)
Cop M 1872-1900 (MCMI)
Cop (Mf) C 1871-1948, M 1872-1962, B 1872-1972 (CRO)

CROWTON (Primitive Methodist) b 1840, closed 1976

CROXTON township in Middlewich (43)

CUDDINGTON township in Malpas (260)

CUDDINGTON township in Weaverham (277)

CULCHETH New Church chapelry in Lancashire, transferred to Cheshire, 1974 *see* Lancashire NIPR

DANE BRIDGE St Paul created a parish in 1846 from Davenham and Witton, abolished 1930
OR C 1846-1967, M 1849-1963, B 1849-1905 (CRO)
BT index CB 1890 (CRO)
Cop B 1849-1956 (Ptd, Northwich Group of Family History Society of Cheshire, 1994); M 1849-1900 (MCMI); M 1849-79 (FHS of Cheshire)

DARESBURY All Saints (143) chapelry in Runcorn created a parish in 1738 [Bucklow Hundred; Northwich Union]
OR C 1617-1951, M 1617-1975, B 1617-1941 (CRO)
BT 1600, 1605-08, 1610-13, 1616-22, 1624-25, 1628, 1632-36, 1639-41, 1663, 1665-66, 1668-69, 1671-76, 1678-85, 1690-91, 1693-1701, 1703-08, 1710-20, 1722-39, 1741-44, 1746-1814, 1816-55 (CRO)
Cop 1600-1724 (OR and BT) (Ms CRO); C 1617-1809, M 1620-1795, B 1617-1809 (Chester City Lib); M 1701-20, 1786-1818, 1825-37 (CMI)
Cop (Mf) C 1617-1951, M 1617-1949, B 1617-1941 (CRO, Manchester Local Hist Lib)

DARESBURY Moore (Wesleyan Methodist) b 1812, reb 1870 (K 1928)

DARNHALL township in Whitegate (198)

DAVENHAM St Wilfrid (4,515) [Northwich Hundred; Congleton Union]
OR C 1560-1943, M 1560-1977, Banns 1754-1806, 1823-50, B 1560-1937 (CRO)
BT 1588, 1593, 1600, 1604, 1608, 1610-14, 1617-20, 1623-25, 1627-30, 1632-35, 1637-38, 1641, 1657-76, 1679-99, 1701-1850, 1852-55, 1857, 1859-84 (CRO)
Cop M 1700-1900 (MCMI); M 1754-1812 (Ms CRO); M 1813-37 (NCMI); M 1665-77, 1708-21, 1744-1805, 1821-37 (CMI)
Cop (Mf) C 1560-1888, M 1560-1913, B 1560-1903 (CRO, Manchester Local Hist Lib, Northwich Lib); C 1877-78, 1883-88, M 1560-1623, 1665-1794, B 1797-1812, 1877-78, 1883-88 (SG)

DAVENHAM Trinity Chapel (Wesleyan Methodist) b 1819, reb 1888, *fl.* 1976

DAVENHAM Shirlach (United Methodist) b 1846, *fl.* 1972

DAVENHAM Hartford Road (Primitive Methodist) b 1852, closed 1962
OR M 1924-57 (CRO)

DAVENHAM (Independent) (K 1928)

DAVENHAM Preston on the Hill (Primitive Methodist) (K 1928)

DAVENPORT township in Astbury transferred to Swettenham, 1880 (103)

DELAMARE St Peter (828) extra-parochial place, part of Delamere Forest, created a parish in 1812 [Eddisbury Hundred; Northwich Union]
OR C 1817-1975, M 1818-1991, B 1820-1948 (CRO)
BT 1817-31, 1876 (+ index CB 1876) (CRO)
Cop M 1818-1900 (MCMI); M 1817-37 (NCMI); M 1818-38 (CMI)
Cop (Mf) C 1817-1918, M 1818-1919, B 1820-1905 (CRO)

DELAMARE (Presbyterian) b 1816 (K 1928)

DELAMARE (Wesleyan Methodist) b 1913

DELAMARE (United Methodist) (K 1928)

DISLEY St Mary (2,037) chapelry in Stockport created a parish in 1741
[Macclesfield Hundred; Hayfield Union]
OR C 1591-1962, M 1591-1738, 1838-1980, Banns 1925-51, 1972-88, B 1591-1958 (CRO)
BT 1604, 1619-23, 1664-85, 1689-92, 1694-95, 1697-1701, 1710, 1712-1802, 1804-57 (CRO)
Cop 1592-1727 (Manchester Central Lib); M 1591-1739 (Ptd, Phil 1, 1909); M 1651-75, 1701-50 (Boyd); M 1651-1750 (NCMI); M 1592-1606, 1727-35, 1738-44 (CMI)
Cop (Mf) C 1591-1962, M 1591-1964, B 1591-1958 (CRO, Manchester Local Hist Lib)

DISLEY (Wesleyan Methodist) f 1805, reb 1906 (K 1928)

DISLEY Furness Vale (United Methodist) reb 1884

DISLEY Buxton Road (Baptist) b 1893, *fl.*1989

DITTON St Michael chapelry in Lancs, transferred to Cheshire, 1974 *see* Lancashire NIPR

DODCOTT cum WILKESLEY township part in Audlem, part in Wrenbury (637)

DODDINGTON St John (37) township in Wybunbury created a parish in 1841
OR CMB 1838+ (Inc)

DODDINGTON Checkley cum Wrinehill (Primitive Methodist) b 1824 (K 1928)

DODDINGTON Bridgemere (Wesleyan Methodist) b 1831 (K 1928)

DODLESTON St Mary (356) [part Broxton Hundred, Cheshire, part Maylor Hundred, Flintshire; Great Boughton Union 1837-53, Hawarden Union 1853-71, Chester Union 1871-1930]
OR C 1570-1903, M 1570-1837, Banns 1754-1812, B 1570-1880 (CRO)
BT 1584, 1586, 1599-1601, 1604, 1608, 1611, 1613, 1617-18, 1624, 1629-33, 1638, 1641,1662-63, 1668, 1670-78, 1680-83, 1685, 1687, 1689-90, 1694-98,1712-16, 1718, 1720-28, 1730, 1732-35, 1737-41, 1743-86, 1788-1803, 1805-47, 1851,1861-72 (CRO)
Cop C 1584-1838, M 1613-1838, B 1599-1838 (BT) (Chester City Lib); 1662-1724 (BT) (Ts CRO, SG); M 1747-1803, 1805-37 (CMI)
Cop (Mf) C 1570-1903, M 1570-1837, B 1570-1880 (CRO, Manchester Local Hist Lib)

DODLESTON (Primitive Methodist) b 1867

DUCKINGTON township in Malpas (66)

DUDDON St Peter (203) township in and chapel of ease to Tarvin
OR M 1900-65, Banns 1902-53, B 1898-1961 (CRO); C 1896+ (Inc)
Cop CB 1896-1907 (CRO)

DUKINFIELD Cemetery (40 acres)

DUKINFIELD St John the Evangelist (14, 681) created a parish in 1841 from Stockport
[Macclesfield Hundred; Ashton under Lyne Union]
OR C 1841-1946, M 1842-1940, B 1841-1955 (CRO)
BT 1844-54 (CRO)
Cop (Mf) C 1841-1910, M 1842-1906, B 1841-1955 (CRO)

DUKINFIELD St Mark, Church Street created a parish from Stockport in 1846
OR C 1846-1917, M 1849-1924 (CRO)
BT 1846-51, 1882-1903 (+ index C 1882-91) (CRO)
Cop (Mf) C 1846-1900, M 1849-1905 (CRO)

DUKINFIELD St Luke, King Street created a parish 1906 from St John and St Mark
OR CMB 1875+ (Inc)

DUKINFIELD alias STALYBRIDGE Christ Church created a parish in 1880 from St John, Ashton under Lyne and New Stalybridge St George
OR C 1879-1976, M 1880-1975 (CRO)
BT 1892 (CRO)

DUKINFIELD Providence Chapel, Dukinfield Hall (Independent) f 17th century (K 1928)
OR C 1676-1713, 1762-1840, M 1677-1713, B 1676-1713, 1761-93, 1836-38 (location unknown); ZC 1806-37, B 1807-37 (PRO: RG 4/179-181)
Cop M 1677-1713 (Ptd, *North Cheshire Family Historian* 9 (1), 1982);
Extr CMB 1677-1713 (Ptd, *Transactions of the Historic Society of Lancashire and Cheshire* 33, 1881); M 1677-1713 (NCMI)
Cop (Mf) C 1676-1713, 1762-1840, M 1677-1713, B 1676-1713, 1761-93, 1836-38 (Manchester Local Hist Lib, Tameside Lib); ZC 1806-37, B 1807-37 (CRO, Manchester Local Hist Lib, SLC)

DUKINFIELD Chapel Hill (Unitarian) f 1707, reb 1840 (K 1928)

DUKINFIELD Old Road (Moravian) f 1724, b 1755 (K 1928)
OR ZC 1785-85, 1812-49, B 1825-40 (PRO: RG 4/97) (ZCB 1786-1812 are in the register of Fairfield, Lancashire PRO RG 4/3122)
Cop (Mf) ZC 1785-85, 1812-49, B 1825-40 (CRO, Tameside Lib)

DUKINFIELD St Mary, Zetland Street (Roman Catholic) b 1825, reb 1854 (K 1928)

DUKINFIELD Foundry Road (Wesleyan Methodist: Ashton under Lyme Circuit) (Lewis 1831) (K 1928)

DUKINFIELD Foundry Street (Primitive Methodist) f 1836, b 1877 (K 1928)

DUKINFIELD Bethesda Chapel, Wellington Street (United Methodist: Ashton Circuit) b 1840

DUKINFIELD Astley Street (Primitive Methodist) b 1872 (K 1928)

DUKINFIELD Crescent Road (Independent) *fl.*1892 (K 1928)

DUKINFIELD Oxford Road (Baptist) f 1904, *fl.*1989

DUKINFIELD Spiritualist Church, Railway Street (K 1928)

DUNHAM MASSEY St Margaret (1,105) township in Bowdon, created a parish in 1855
OR C 1855-1935, M 1856-1932, Banns 1907-25 (CRO)
BT 1855-68, 1895-1901 (CRO)
Cop (Mf) C 1855-1915, M 1856-1918 (CRO)

DUNHAM MASSEY St Mark
OR C 1866-1915, M 1867-1983, Banns 1866-1945, B 1921-53 (CRO)
BT 1873-93, 1896-1913 (+ index C 1873-93) (CRO)
Cop (Mf) C 1866-1915, M 1867-1971 (CRO)

DUNHAM on the HILL St Luke (322) township in Thornton le Moors created a parish in 1888
OR M 1868-77 (CRO); CB 1868+, M 1877+ (Inc)

DUTTON township in Great Budworth (329)

EASTHAM St Mary, New Chester Road (1,644) [Wirral Hundred; Wirral Union]
OR C 1598-1866, M 1598-1838, Banns 1754-1812, 1823-67, B 1598-1884 (CRO)
BT 1600, 1602-04, 1606-10, 1615, 1617-19, 1621-24, 1626-27, 1630-32, 1634, 1636, 1638-39, 1641, 1663-64, 1668-77, 1679-85, 1690-91, 1694-1736, 1741-46, 1749-61, 1764-92, 1793-1830, 1832-70 (CRO)
Cop 1598-1700 (Ptd, F. Sanders, 1891); 1701-38 (CRO); 1598-1644, 1653-90 (Liverpool Ref Lib); M 1749-55, 1794-1830, 1832-37 (CMI)
Cop (Mf) C 1598-1866, M 1598-1838, B 1598-1884 (CRO, Wirral Archives, Manchester Local Hist Lib)

EASTHAM St David, Crosthwaite Avenue (United Reformed Church) f 1943, *fl.* 1991

EATON Christ Church (525) township in Astbury, created a parish in 1858
OR C 1857-1937, Banns 1858-1947, B 1858-1978 (CRO); M 1858+ (Inc)
BT 1858-96 (+ index CB 1873-88) (CRO)

EATON St Thomas (502) township in Tarporley, created a parish in 1896
OR CM 1896+ (Inc)

EATON township in Davenham (13)

EATON township in Eccleston (73)

ECCLESTON St Mary (361) [Broxton Hundred; Great Boughton Union 1837-53, Hawarden Union 1853-71, Chester Union 1871-1930] united to Pulford, 1973
OR C 1593-1892, M 1593-1833, Banns 1754-1812, B 1593-1885 (CRO)
BT 1599, 1603-04, 1610, 1614, 1617, 1623, 1631-34, 1638-39, 1663, 1666-71, 1675-79, 1681-84, 1704-32, 1734-59, 1761-79, 1782, 1784-89, 1791-96, 1798-1805, 1807-1905, 1912 (+ index CB 1873-79) (CRO)
Cop 1593-1899 (Ts I CRO); C 1665-99, M 1600-99, B 1599-1699 (Chester City Lib); M 1731-1837 (CMI)
Cop (Mf) C 1593-1892, M 1593-1833, B 1593-1885 (CRO, Manchester Local Hist Lib)

EDDINSHALL township in Chester St Oswald (24)

EDDISBURY township in Delamere (178)

EDGE township in Malpas (310)

EDGERLEY township in Alford (11)

EDLESTON township in Acton (104)

EGERTON township in Malpas (114)

EGREMONT St John otherwise LISCARD, Church Street created a parish in 1884 from Wallasey and Seacombe
OR C 1833-1974, M 1837-1970, Banns 1834-83, 1906-13, 1933-63, 1977-87, B 1833-81 (CRO)
BT 1833-61 (CRO)
Cop (Mf) C 1833-1901, M 1837-1907 (CRO)

EGREMONT St Columba *see* **LISCARD St Columba**

EGREMONT Seabrook Road (Presbyterian, later United Reformed Church) f 1859 b 1908, *fl.*1991

EGREMONT Falkland Road later (1892) Liscard Road (Baptist) f 1850, b 1868, *fl.*1989

EGREMONT Synagogue, Falkland Road (Jewish) b 1868, became Jewish, 1911 (K 1924)

EGREMONT Crescent Road (Church of Christ) (K 1946)

ELLESMERE PORT Christ Church created a parish in 1871 from Eastham
OR C 1844-1965, M 1872-1993, Banns 1956-70, B 1844-1941 (CRO)
BT 1851, 1866-68, 1891-92 (CRO)

ELLESMERE PORT (Primitive Methodist)
OR C 1873-1932 (Circuit) (CRO)

ELLESMERE PORT Our Lady Star of the Sea, Enfield Road (Roman Catholic) f 1909

ELLESMERE PORT Chester Road (Independent, later United Reformed Church) f 1926, *fl.*1991

ELLESMERE PORT Upper Mersey Street later (1900) Queen Street (Primitive Methodist) b 1872, closed 1968
OR M 1909-60 (CRO)

ELLESMERE PORT Whitby (Primitive Methodist) b 1873, reb 1968

ELLESMERE PORT Trinity Chapel, King Street b 1906, reb in Whitby Road 1914
OR C 1907-47 (CRO)

ELLESMERE PORT Grace Road (Independent) b 1927, closed 1983
OR C 1952-81, M 1952-81, B 1951-84 (CRO)

ELLESMERE PORT Pooltown Chapel, Rivacre Road (Primitive Methodist) b 1901, destroyed 1950, reopened in Rossmore Road West, 1955
OR C 1932-47 (CRO)

ELLESMERE PORT Heathfield Road (Primitive Methodist) b 1909, closed 1963
OR C 1909-22, 1930-37 (CRO)

ELLESMERE PORT Wolverham Society (Methodist) f 1954, closed 1962
OR C 1957-62 (CRO)

ELLESMERE PORT St Saviour, Tarporley Road (Roman Catholic) f 1959

ELLESMERE PORT Westminster Chapel (Methodist) b 1967

ELTON township in Thornton le Moors (210)

ELTON township in Warmingham (430)

ELWORTH St Peter created a parish from Sandbach and Warmingham, 1847
OR C 1846-1915, M 1847-1917, B 1846-1925 (CRO)
Cop (Mf) C 1846-1915, M 1847-1917, B 1846-1925 (CRO, Manchester Local Hist Lib)

ELWORTH Mount Pleasant Chapel (United Methodist) f 1861, b 1889, *fl.*1975

ELWORTH The Avenue Chapel (Wesleyan Methodist) b 1912 (K 1928)

ELWORTH Bradwall (Wesleyan Methodist) (K 1928)

ETCHELLS, NORTHERN township in Northenden (1,443)

ETCHELLS, STOCKPORT township in Stockport

FADDILEY township in Acton (316)

FALLIBROOME township in Prestbury (35)

FARNDON St Chad (864) [Broxton Hundred; Great Boughton Union; Tarvin Union 1871-1930]
OR C 1603-1906, M 1603-1961, Banns 1754-1812, 1824-95, B 1603-1887 (CRO)
BT 1611, 1613-17, 1622-24, 1627-39, 1632-33, 1641, 1662-63, 1666-71, 1673-85, 1689-1908 (+ index CB 1873-91) (CRO)
Cop C 1785-1812 (Ptd, Index *Family History Society of Cheshire Journal* 3-4, 1972-73, *Cheshire Family Historian* 6 (3), 1977); C 1813-37 (Ptd, Index *Family History Society of Cheshire Journal* 1 (2-4), 1970); M 1756-1837 (CMI)
Cop (Mf) C 1603-1906, M 1603-1961, B 1603-1850 (CRO, Manchester Local Hist Lib)

FARNDON Churton (Primitive Methodist) b 1833 (K 1928)

FARNDON Barton (Independent, later United Reformed Church) b 1877, *fl.* 1991

FARNDON Rock Chapel, Church Street (Independent, later United Reformed Church) f 1889, *fl.* 1991

FARNWORTH St Luke ancient parish in Lancashire, transferred to Cheshire, 1974 *see* Lancashire NIPR

FERNILEE Holy Trinity *see* Derbyshire NIPR

FOREST CHAPEL *see* **MACCLESFIELD FOREST**

FRANKBY St John the Divine (114) township in West Kirby and Thurstaston created a parish, 1861
OR C 1862-1963, B 1862-1983 (CRO); M 1862+ (Inc)
BT 1862-1908 (+ index CB 1873-86, B 1887) (CRO)
Cop C 1962-1941, 1946-47 (CRO)
Cop (Mf) C 1862-1963, B 1862-1983 (CRO, Wirral Archives, Manchester Local Hist Lib)

FRIEZLAND Christ Church created a parish in 1848 from Saddleworth and Lydgate both in West Yorkshire and Stalybridge St Paul
OR CM 1848+ (Inc)

FRODSHAM St Lawrence (5,547) (Borough) [Eddisbury Hundred; Runcorn Union]
OR C 1558-1963, M 1558-1951, Banns 1806-1916, B 1558-1952 (CRO)
BT 1603, 1606-08, 1610-11, 1613-14, 1617-19, 1621-23, 1625, 1627-29, 1631-37, 1639-40, 1660, 1662-63, 1665-76, 1678-82, 1684, 1690-1726, 1728-39, 1742-1824, 1826-77 (+ index CB 1873-77) (CRO)
Cop 1558-1812 (Ptd, I.E. Jermyn, 3 vols., 1908-13); B 1813-1982 (Ts I CRO); M 1558-1812 (NCMI); M 1789-1826 (CMI)
Cop (Mf) C 1558-1928, M 1558-1921, B 1558-1899 (CRO, Manchester Local Hist Lib); MB 1558-1812 (SG)

FRODSHAM St Dunstan, Main Street chapel of ease with no separate registers

FRODSHAM Trinity Chapel, Chapel Lane later (1873) Main Street (Wesleyan Methodist) f 1823, b 1873
OR C 1844-87, 1951-62 (Circuit), M 1874-96 (CRO)

FRODSHAM Rock Chapel, Main Street (United Methodist) b 1837, closed 1937
OR C 1894-1913 (Circuit) (CRO)

FRODSHAM Manley (Primitive Methodist) b 1859, closed *c*1970
OR C 1899-1965 (Circuit) (CRO)

FRODSHAM Bourne Chapel, Main Street (Primitive Methodist) b 1877, *fl.*1948

FRODSHAM Five Crosses, Overton (Wesleyan Methodist) b 1885, *fl.*1985

FRODSHAM Union Chapel, Bridge Lane (Independent and Baptist, later United Reformed Church) b 1886, *fl.*1991

FRODSHAM Sutton Weaver Chapel (Wesleyan Methodist) b 1893, closed 1965

FRODSHAM St Luke, Ship Street (Roman Catholic) f 1949

FRODSHAM Newton Hall Chapel (Wesleyan Methodist) b 1951, closed 1983
OR M 1951-83 (CRO)

FULSHAW township in Wilmslow (291)

FURNESS VALE St John chapel of ease to Disley

GATLEY St James the Apostle created a parish in 1882 from Stockport St Thomas
OR M 1882-1932 (CRO); CB 1881+ (Inc)
BT 1881-97, 1899 (+ index C 1881-90) (CRO)

GATLEY (Independent) f 1778, demolished 1967
OR C 1779-1944, B 1823-1950 (Manchester Local Hist Lib)
Cop B 1777-1967 (Ts I CRO, SG)

GAWSWORTH St James (847) [Macclesfield Hundred; Macclesfield Union]
OR C 1557-1885, M 1557-1987, Banns 1941-70, B 1557-1860 (CRO)
BT 1586, 1590, 1600, 1623-24, 1630-31, 1635-41, 1662, 1664-65, 1667-69, 1671-72, 1675-85, 1687, 1691-1833, 1835-39, 1841-42, 1851, 1867-68 (CRO)
Cop 1557-1837 (Ptd, R. Dickinson, 1955); M 1557-1812 (Ptd, Phil 1, 1909); M 1557-1812 (Boyd); M 1557-1837 (NCMI); M 1765-1837 (CMI)

GAWSWORTH The Warren (Wesleyan Methodist) b 1892, *fl.*1954

GAYTON township in Heswall

GEE CROSS Holy Trinity created a parish in 1880 from Compstall, Hyde St George and Hyde St Thomas
OR CMB 1891+ (Inc)
BT 1891-1902 (+ index CB 1889-91) (CRO)

GLAZEBURY All Saints chapelry in Lancashire, transferred to Cheshire, 1974

GODLEY cum NEWTON GREEN St John the Baptist (636) township in Mottram, created a parish in 1847
OR C 1847-1909, M 1850-1963, B 1850-1906 (CRO)
BT 1847-72 (CRO)

GOLBORNE BELLOW township in Tattenhall (96)

GOLBORNE DAVID township in Handley (80)

GOOSTREY cum BARNSHAW St Luke (292) township and chapelry in Sandbach, created a parish in 1724 [Northwich Hundred; Congleton Union]
OR C 1561-1964, M 1561-1940, Banns 1773-1863, B 1561-1949 (CRO)
BT 1576, 1596, 1600, 1607, 1611, 1618, 1620, 1622-23, 1626, 1628-29, 1634-35, 1637?, 1658-66, 1668-76, 1679-81, 1683-85, 1690-91, 1694-96, 1699-1706, 1708, 1711-12, 1714-15, 1717-67, 1770-1860 (CRO)
Cop C 1561-1795, M 1562-1785, B 1562-1810 (Chester AS); C 1561-1837, MB 1561-1900 (Ts CRO); M 1754-1837 (NCMI); M 1717-55, 1772-1837 (CMI)
Cop (Mf) C 1561-1904, M 1561-1940, B 1561-1949 (CRO, Manchester Local Hist Lib)

GOOSTREY cum BARNSHAW (Wesleyan Methodist) b 1875, *fl.*1975

GRAFTON township in Tilston (18)

GRANGE alias CALDYGRANGE St Andrew, Runcorn (created from West Kirby)
OR M 1965-82 (CRO); C 1965+ (Inc)

GRAPPENHALL St Wilfrid (2,607) [Bucklow Hundred; Runcorn Union 1836-45, Warrington Union 1845-1930]
OR C 1574-1942, M 1574-1942, Banns 1856-1932, B 1574-1925 (CRO)
BT 1596, 1606-08, 1610, 1613, 1617-19, 1621-24, 1627, 1630-31, 1633-34, 1636-37, 1639, 1641, 1658-60, 1663, 1665-66, 1668-76, 1678-85, 1690-1705, 1707-39, 1741-1890 (+ index CB 1873-90) (CRO)
Cop C 1574-1839,M 1574-1832,B 1573-1831 (Chester AS); M 1744-57, 1799-1837 (CMI)
Cop (Mf) C 1574-1917, M 1574-1920, B 1574-1925 (CRO, Manchester Local Hist Lib)

GREASBY St Nicholas township part in Thurstaston, part in West Kirby (141)

GREASBY (Methodist) b 1936, *fl.*1960

GREASBY Our Lady of Pity, Mill Land (Roman Catholic) f 1940

GREASBY Wirral School Chapel (Wesleyan Methodist: Hoylake and West Kirby Circuit)

GUILDEN SUTTON St John the Evangelist (132) [Broxton Hundred; Great Boughton Union 1837-71, Tarvin Union 1871-1930]
OR C 1645-1932, M 1661-1967, Banns 1755-1812, 1825-63, B 1595-1952 (CRO)
BT 1602, 1605, 1608-09, 1613-14, 1616, 1618, 1622-25, 1627, 1629, 1631, 1637, 1641, 1666, 1670-72, 1674-85, 1696-1704, 1706, 1715-18, 1721, 1723-24, 1727-31, 1733-39, 1741-42, 1744-53, 1758-60, 1762-73, 1775-77, 1779-1826, 1828-55 (CRO)
Cop C 1645-1726, M 1661-1721, B 1595-1722 (Ptd, *Cheshire Sheaf* Series 4, Volume 1, 1966); CMB 1727-1812 (Ms CRO); M 1680-1721, 1744-53, 1756-1837 (CMI)
Cop (Mf) C 1595-1932, M 1595-1967, B 1595-1952 (CRO, Manchester Local Hist Lib); C 1645-1781, M 1661-1880, B 1595-1880 (SG)

GUILDEN SUTTON (Primitive Methodist) b 1873 (K 1928)

HALE St Mary (near Widnes) ancient parish in Lancashire, transferred to Cheshire, 1974 *see* Lancashire NIPR

HALE St Peter (945) township in Bowdon, created a parish in 1906 from Bowdon and Altrincham St John the Evangelist
OR C 1892-1930, M 1897-1939, Banns 1897-1940 (CRO)
BT 1906-14 (C only) (CRO)

HALEBARNS St Paul (created from Altrincham)
OR M 1917-65 (CRO); CB 1917+ (Inc)

HALTON Cemetery (opened 1885; 1 acre)

HALTON St Mary the Virgin (1,322) chapelry in Runcorn, created a parish in 1718 [Bucklow Hundred; Runcorn Union]
OR C 1732-1971, M 1732-1979, Banns 1863-1947 (CRO)
BT 1732-39, 1741-1841, 1843-45, 1851-87 (+ index C 1872-87) (CRO)
Cop M 1732-39 (CMI)
Cop (Mf) C 1732-1940, M 1732-1812 (CRO, Manchester Local Hist Lib)

HALTON (Wesleyan Methodist) f 1818, b 1875 (K 1928)

HALTON (Primitive Methodist) b 1882 (K 1928)

HAMPTON township in Malpas (273)

HANDFORTH St Chad (1,980) township in Cheadle, created a parish in 1877
OR C 1840-1941 (CRO); M 1840+ (Inc)

HANDFORTH Kilham Chapel (United Methodist) b 1850

HANDFORTH St Mary, Wilmslow Road (Wesleyan Methodist) b 1872 (K 1928)

HANDLEY All Saints (389) [Broxton Hundred; Great Boughton Union 1837-71, Tarvin Union 1871-1930]
OR C 1570-1880, M 1570-1981, Banns 1754-1808, B 1570-1948 (CRO)
BT 1596, 1599, 1601, 1604-06, 1610, 1613-15, 1618, 1622-31, 1633-35, 1639-42, 1660-71, 1673-77, 1679-85, 1690, 1692, 1694, 1697, 1700, 1708, 1710-11, 1715-16, 1718-19, 1721-23, 1725-47, 1749-1831, 1833-1905 (+ index CB 1873-90) (CRO)
Cop M 1660-71, 1725-1813 (CMI)

HANKELOW township in Audlem (289)

HAPSFORD township in Thornton le Moors (83)

HARGRAVE St Peter chapelry, created a parish in 1878 from Tarvin and Waverton
OR C 1744-1883, M 1746-49, B 1744-1812 (CRO); B 1813+ (Inc)
BT 1632-35, 1637, 1639-41, 1666, 1668, 1671-72, 1676-78, 1680-85, 1806-49, 1851-69, 1883-89 (+ index CB 1883-89) (CRO)
Cop M 1828-32, 1835-36 (CMI)

HARGRAVE (Wesleyan Methodist) b 1859, closed 1981

HARGRAVE Huxley (Primitive Methodist) (K 1928)

HARTFORD St John the Baptist (863) chapelry part in Great Budworth, part in Weaverham, created a parish in 1825 from Witton
OR C 1846-1941, M 1837-1943 (CRO); B 1846+ (Inc)
Cop M 1837-1900 (MCMI)

HARTFORD (Wesleyan Methodist) f 1833, b 1891, *fl.* 1983

HARTHILL All Saints (166) [Broxton Hundred; Great Boughton Union 1837-71, Tarvin Union 1871-1930]
OR C 1730-1812, M 1736-1830, Banns 1804-12, B 1730-1812 (CRO); CB 1813+ (Inc)
BT 1599, 1601, 1604, 1606, 1610, 1613-14, 1618, 1622-29, 1631, 1633, 1635, 1639, 1641, 1664, 1666, 1669-71, 1673-76, 1679-85, 1687, 1690-92, 1694-95, 1721, 1723-60, 1762-1898, 1900-13 (+ index CB 1873-91) (CRO)
Cop M 1599-1837 (Ts CRO, SG, NCMI); M 1746-72, 1801-37 (CMI)

HASLINGTON St Matthew (1,028) chapelry in Barthomley, created a parish in 1766 [Nantwich Hundred; Nantwich Union]
OR C 1645-1907, M 1652-53, 1676, 1687, 1715-53, 1841-1926, B 1645-1715, 1773-1899 (CRO)
BT 1665, 1667, 1673, 1812-76 (+ index CB 1873-76) (CRO)
Cop M 1716-53, 1761 (CMI)
Cop (Mf) C 1645-1907, M 1645-1773, 1841-1926, B 1645-1899 (CRO, Manchester Local Hist Lib)

HASLINGTON (Independent, later United Reformed Church) b 1810, *fl.* 1991

HASLINGTON Winterley Chapel b 1834 (Primitive Methodist)

HASLINGTON Oakhanger Chapel (Primitive Methodist) f 1830s, b 1868, *fl.* 1975

HASLINGTON (Free Gospel) b 1870 (K 1928)

HASLINGTON (Baptist) f 1884, b 1887, closed 1971
OR M 1908-71 (CRO)

HASLINGTON (Wesleyan Methodist) b 1909, *fl.* 1977

HASSALL township in Sandbach (200)

HATHERTON township in Wybunbury (447)

HATTERSLEY St Barnabas Apostle and Martyr (477) township in Mottram, created a parish in 1966

HATTON St Luke chapel of ease to Daresbury, township in Runcorn (391)

HATTON township in Waverton (150)

HAUGHTON St Anne created a parish in 1881 from Denton Christ Church, Lancs and Stockport

HAZEL GROVE *see* **NORBURY**

HEALD GREEN St Catherine created a parish in 1958 from Gatley and Handforth
OR CM 1958+ (Inc)

HELSBY St Paul (534) township in Frodsham, created a parish in 1875
OR C 1870-1926, M 1876-1954, B 1871-1924 (CRO)
BT 1870-1902 (+ index B 1876, CB 1877-80, C 1881-83) (CRO)

HELSBY Trinity Chapel (Wesleyan Methodist) b 1853, closed 1960
OR M 1931-58 (CRO)

HELSBY Zion later Central Chapel (United Methodist) b 1858, *fl.* 1965

HELSBY The Avenue Chapel (Primitive Methodist) b 1902, closed 1965

HELSBY St Mary Magdalen, Upper Rake Lane (Roman Catholic) f 1961

HENBURY cum PEXALL St Thomas (421) township in Prestbury, created a parish in 1851
OR C 1845-1971 (CRO); MB 1845+ (Inc)
BT 1892-1904 (CRO)

HENHULL township in Acton (62)

HESWALL St Peter (406) [Wirral Hundred; Wirral Union]
OR C 1559-1945, M 1559-1963, Banns 1754-1812, B 1558-1946 (CRO)
BT 1586, 1601, 1604-05, 1608-10, 1615, 1619, 1621-22, 1636, 1638, 1666, 1668-69, 1672, 1674-77, 1679-85, 1688, 1690-91, 1693-95, 1698-1701, 1703-04, 1706-12, 1715-30, 1732-35, 1737-39, 1741-72, 1774-79, 1781-1803, 1805-78, 1892-1907 (+ index CB 1873-78, 1892-93) (CRO)
Cop 1559-1729 (Ptd, T.H. May, 1896); M 1754-1839 (CMI)
Cop (Mf) C 1559-1945, M 1559-1963, B 1558-1946 (CRO, Wirral Archives, Manchester Local Hist Lib)

HESWALL Good Shepherd chapel of ease to Heswall St Peter
OR CM 1901+ (Inc)

HESWALL Centenary Chapel, Milner Road later Telegraph Road (Wesleyan Methodist: Birkenhead Circuit) f 1859, b 1891 (K 1946)
OR C 1859-1949 (CRO)

HESWALL Telegraph Road (Presbyterian, later United Reformed Church) b 1909, *fl.* 1991

HESWALL Our Lady and St John, Telegraph Road (Roman Catholic) f 1919

HESWALL Meeting House (Society of Friends) f 1939

HIGH LANE St Thomas created a parish in 1860 from Poynton with Worth, Marple, Stockport and Norbury
OR Banns 1861-1982 (CRO); CM 1860+ (Inc)

HOCKENHULL township in Tarvin (35)

HOLLINFARE St Helen ancient parish in Lancashire, transferred to Cheshire, 1974
see Lancashire NIPR

HOLLINGWORTH St Mary (1,760) township in Mottram created a parish in 1922 from Tintwistle
OR CMB 1864+ (Inc)

HOLLINGWORTH (Independent) b 1865 (K 1928)

HOLLINGWORTH (Methodist New Connexion) f 1830 (K 1928)
OR ZC 1812, 1830-37 (PRO: RG 4/170)
Cop (Mf) ZC 1812, 1830-37 (CRO, SLC)

HOOLE All Saints or **CHESTER All Saints**, Hoole (249) township part in Plemstall, part in Chester St John, created a parish in 1872 from Chester Christ Church
OR C 1868-1979, M 1872-1985, Banns 1976-91 (CRO)
BT 1868-94, 1896-98, 1900-06 (+ index CB 1873-93) (CRO)

HOOLE Walker Street (Independent) f 1887, *fl.* 1972
OR C 1908-57 (Chester RO)

HOOLE Hamilton Street (Primitive Methodist) b 1928 (K 1928)

HOOSE township in West Kirby (196), created a parish in 1839 as **HOYLAKE Holy Trinity** (q.v.)

HOOTON St Paul (103) township in Eastham, created a parish in 1862
OR C 1862-1946, M 1863-1968, Banns 1863-1968 (CRO)
BT 1892-93, 1897-1901 (CRO)

HOOTON St Mary of the Angels (Roman Catholic) f 1866, b 1879 (K 1928)

HOOTON Little Sutton (Presbyterian) b 1838

HOOTON Little Sutton (Wesleyan Methodist) b 1840 (K 1928)

HORTON township in Tilston (148)

HORTON cum PEEL township in Tarvin (36)

HOUGH township in Wybunbury (252)

HOYLAKE Holy Trinity township in West Kirby, created a parish in 1839 as Hoose, renamed 1860
OR C 1834-1919, M 1834-1952, Banns 1834-44, 1962-1908, B 1834-1921 (CRO)
BT 1836-42, 1871-88, 1893-1911 (+ index CB 1873-88) (CRO)
Cop M 1834-37 (CMI)
Cop (Mf) C 1834-1903, M 1834-1912, Banns 1834-44, 1962-1908, B 1834-1910 (CRO)

HOYLAKE St Hildeburgh chapel of ease to Holy Trinity b 1899
OR M 1899-1950 (CRO); CB 1899+ (Inc)

HOYLAKE Filey Terrace, Station Road (Independent) f 1874, reb 1906, closed 1987

HOYLAKE St Luke, Market Street (Wesleyan Methodist: Hoylake and West Kirby Circuit) f 1884, b 1907, closed 1963
OR C 1884-1948 (CRO)

HOYLAKE Alderley Road (Presbyterian)
OR C 1908+, M 1910+, B 1887+ (Ch Sec)
Cop C 1908-80, M 1910-80, B 1887-1980 (Ts CRO)

HOYLAKE Meeting House (Society of Friends) f 1898

HOYLAKE St Catherine and St Martina, Birkenhead Road, Meols (Roman Catholic) f 1928

HULME, CHURCH alias HOLMES CHAPEL St Luke chapelry in Sandbach, created a parish in 1733 [Northwich Hundred; Congleton Union]
OR C 1613-1841, M 1613-1837, Banns 1754-1812, 1840-78, B 1613-1903 (CRO)
BT 1576, 1590, 1600, 1604, 1608-09, 1611, 1613-15, 1617-20, 1621 or 1623?, 1622, 1624-26, 1629, 1632-35, 1658-60, 1663, 1666-76, 1679-83, 1685-97, 1699-1761, 1763-66, 1768-88, 1790-1821, 1823-24, 1826-28, 1830-41, 1855-98 (+ index CB 1873-79) (CRO)
Cop 1682-1837 (SG); M 1738-1837 (NCMI); M 1717-1837 (CMI)
Cop (Mf) C 1613-1841, M 1613-1837, B 1613-1903 (CRO, Manchester Local Hist Lib)

HULME, CHURCH (Wesleyan Methodist) b 1900 (K 1928)

HULME, CHURCH (United Methodist) b 1851 (K 1928)

HULME WALFIELD St Michael (109) township in Astbury, created a parish in 1878
OR CMB 1852+ (Inc)
BT 1878-1916 (+ index CB 1873-91) (CRO)

HULME WALFIELD (Primitive Methodist later Wesleyan Methodist) b 1835 (K 1928)

HULME WALFIELD Somerford Booths (Primitive Methodist) (K 1928)

HULSE township in Great Budworth (55)

HUNSTERTON township in Wybunbury (226)

HUNTINGTON township in Chester St Oswald (112)

HURDSFIELD Holy Trinity (3,083) township in Prestbury, created a parish in 1813
OR C 1839-1927, M 1839-1969, B 1839-1940 (CRO)
Cop (Mf) C 1839-1927, M 1839-1930, B 1839-1940 (CRO, Macclesfield Lib, Manchester Local Hist Lib)

HURDSFIELD Fence School Chapel, Waterloo Street (United Methodist) b 1841
OR C 1878-1965, M 1960-65 (CRO)

HURDSFIELD Ebenezer Chapel, Rainow Road (United Methodist) b 1865, *fl.* 1976

HURLESTON township in Acton (198)

HUXLEY township in Waverton (246)

HYDE Cemetery (opened 1894; 24 acres)

HYDE St George created a parish in 1843 from Stockport
OR C 1832-1971, M 1832-1983, B 1832-1973 (CRO)
Cop (Mf) C 1832-1892, M 1832-1900, B 1832-1899 (CRO, Manchester Local Hist Lib)

HYDE St Thomas (7,144) chapelry in Stockport, created a parish in 1846
OR C 1847-1924, M 1868-1919, B 1869-1900 (CRO)
BT 1851, 1868-71 (CRO)
Cop (Mf) C 1847-1924, M 1868-1919, B 1869-1900 (CRO, Manchester Local Hist Lib)

HYDE St John *see* **GODLEY**

HYDE St Mary *see* **NEWTON IN MOTTRAM**

HYDE Chapel (Unitarian) f 1708, reb 1846 (K 1928)

HYDE Hoviley Brow (Primitive Methodist) b 1813 (K 1928)

HYDE Union Street (Independent) f 1814, b 1822, reb 1843 (K 1928)
OR ZC 1822-37 (PRO: RG 4/2150)
Cop (Mf) ZC 1822-37 (CRO, Manchester Local Hist Lib, SLC)

HYDE New Street Chapel (Wesleyan Methodist) f 1823
OR ZC 1820-37 (PRO: RG 4/666)
Cop (Mf) ZC 1820-37 (CRO, SLC)

HYDE Norfolk Street (Wesleyan Methodist) (Lewis 1831) b 1850 (K 1928)

HYDE Zion Chapel, Stockport Road (Independent) b 1847 (K 1928)

HYDE St Paul, St Paul's Street, Newton Moor (Roman Catholic) f 1848 b 1854 (K 1928)

HYDE George Street (United Methodist: Hurst and Hyde Circuit) b 1858 (K 1928)

HYDE Chapel Street later Union Street (Baptist) b 1869, *fl.*1989

HYDE Meeting House, Chapel Street (Society of Friends) b 1873 (K 1928)

HYDE Flowery Field (Unitarian, later undenominational) b 1878 (K 1928)

HYDE Reynold Street (Salvation Army) (K 1928)

HYDE Spiritualist Church, George Street (K 1928)

HYDE Gee Cross (Primitive Methodist) (K 1928)

HYDE Socialist Church, Mottram Road (K 1928)

HYDE Ashton Road (United Methodist: Stalybridge, Newton & Ashton Circuit) (K 1928)

HYDE Newton (United Methodist) (K 1928)

HYDE Rosemount, Newton (Primitive Methodist) (K 1928)

IDDINSHALL township in Chester St Oswald

INCE St James the Great (487) [Eddisbury Hundred; Great Boughton Union 1837-71, Chester Union 1871-1930]
OR C 1687-1786, 1813-70, M 1687-1837, Banns 1754-1810, 1824-1933, B 1687-1786, 1813-1912 (CRO) (early registers lost, but 1687-1774 register recovered in 1857 and 1728-1783 volume recovered between 1867 and 1886)
BT 1600-02, 1605, 1607-08, 1610, 1612-18, 1622-25, 1627, 1629-33, 1635, 1637, 1640-41, 1662-63, 1666, 1668-77, 1679-85, 1688-91, 1694-1707, 1709-36, 1738-80, 1782-98, 1802-03, 1806-58, 1860-85, 1892-98 (+ index CB 1873-85) (CRO)
Cop M 1600-1812 (SG, NCMI); M 1687-1812 (Boyd); M 1709-1837 (CMI)
Cop (Mf) C 1687-1786, 1813-70, M 1687-1837, B 1687-1786, 1813-1912 (CRO, Wirral Archives, Manchester Local Hist Lib)

IRBY township part in Thurstaston, part in Woodchurch (123)

IRBY (Primitive Methodist: Second Circuit) b 1869, reb 1937

IRBY (Wesleyan Methodist: Birkenhead Circuit) b 1933 (K 1946)

KECKWICK township in Runcorn (74)

KELSALL St Philip (648) township in Tarvin, created a parish in 1956
OR C 1868-1962, M 1869-1976, B 1868-1930 (CRO)

KELSALL (Wesleyan Methodist) b 1816, reb 1884, *fl.*1963

KELSALL (Salvation Amry) (K 1928)

KERMINGHAM township in Swettenham (174)

KETTLESHULME township in Prestbury (232)

KINDERTON cum HULME (493) township in Middlewich

KINGSLEY Cemetery (2 acres) (K 1928)

KINGSLEY St John the Evangelist (934) township in Frodsham, created a parish in 1853
OR C 1851-1927, Banns 1851-1914, B 1851-1902 (CRO); M 1851+ (Inc)
Cop M 1851-1900 (MCMI)
BT 1876-83 (+ index CB 1876-83) (CRO)

KINGSLEY Hurst Chapel (Wesleyan Methodist) (Lewis 1831) b 1871, *fl.* 1978

KINGSLEY (United Methodist) b 1843 (K 1928)

KINGSLEY Brookside Chapel (Primitive Methodist) b 1864, closed 1967
OR M 1925-60 (CRO)

KINGS MARSH extra-parochial place, later township in Farndon (70)

KINGSWOOD township in Delamare (86)

KINNERTON, LOWER township in Dodleston (104)

KIRBY, WEST Grange Cemetery, Black Horse Hill (K 1946)

KIRBY, WEST St Bridget, Church Road (1,289) [Wirral Hundred; Wirral Union]
OR C 1561-1964, M 1561-1729, 1754-1959, Banns 1754-1812, 1823-1927, B 1561-1886 (CRO)
BT 1581, 1600, 1604-05, 1609-10, 1614-15, 1617-19, 1621-24, 1626-27, 1630-31, 1636, 1666, 1669, 1671-72, 1674-76, 1679-82, 1684-85, 1690, 1698-1704, 1706-30, 1732, 1734-39, 1741-43, 1746, 1748-1838, 1892-94, 1896-97 (+ index CB 1892-93) (CRO)
Cop 1581-1619 (Ms Index CRO, SG); 1692-1729 (Ts Index CRO); M 1692-1729, 1801-37 (CMI)
Cop (Mf) C 1561-1861, M 1561-1729, 1754-1905, B 1561-1886 (CRO, Wirral Archives, Manchester Local Hist Lib)

KIRBY, WEST St Andrew, Meols Drive created a parish in 1920 from St Bridget
OR CM 1891+ (Inc)

KIRBY, WEST Eaton Road (Primitive Methodist: First Circuit) b 1880, closed 1963

KIRBY, WEST Meols Drive (Presbyterian, later United Reformed Church) f 1890, *fl.* 1991

KIRBY, WEST Grange Road (Welsh Presbyterian) f 1892 (K 1924)

KIRBY, WEST St Agnes, Darmond's Green (Roman Catholic) f 1897

KIRBY, WEST Westbourne Road (Wesleyan Methodist: Hoylake and West Kirby Circuit) b 1903, *fl.* 1981

KIRBY, WEST Free Church, Grange Road later (1928) Brookfield Gardens (Unitarian) f 1910, *fl.* 1969
OR C 1950-53, M 1938-50 (CRO)

KIRBY, WEST Newton cum Larton Chapel (Wesleyan Methodist) b 1914, closed 1972

KIRBY, WEST Meeting House (Society of Friends) b 1940, closed 1948

KNUTSFORD Cemetery, Over Tabley (6 acres) (K 1928)

KNUTSFORD St Helena later St John the Baptist, Church Hill, over King Street (3,599) chapelry in Rostherne, created a parish in 1741 [Bucklow Hundred; Bucklow Union]
OR C 1582-1969, M 1582-1970, Banns 1754-69, B 1582-1972 (CRO)
BT 1581, 1608, 1610, 1617-18, 1620, 1622-25, 1627-30, 1633-34, 1640, 1662-63, 1665-68, 1670-77, 1679-85, 1687-89, 1691-96, 1698-1768, 1770-1815, 1825, 1827-67 (CRO)
Cop M 1813-37 (NCMI); M 1731-46, 1801-37 (CMI)
Cop (Mf) C 1582-1928, M 1582-1924, B 1582-1942 (CRO, Knutsford Lib, Manchester Local Hist Lib)

KNUTSFORD St Cross, Cross Street (217) created a parish in 1858 from Knutsford Over township
OR C 1858-1980, M 1861-1980, Banns 1966-83, B 1858-1968 (CRO)
BT 1858-85 (+ index CB 1873-85) (CRO)

KNUTSFORD Brook Street (Unitarian) f 1672 b 1687 (K 1928)
OR ZCB 1792-1836 (PRO: RG 4/190); ZC 1827-72, M 1840-72, B 1827-72 (CRO) (it is mentioned that the registers 1740-90 disappeared with the minister when he moved to Derbyshire)
Cop ZC 1792-1899, M 1840-99, B 1792-1899 (Ts I CRO)
Cop (Mf) ZCB 1792-1836 (CRO, SLC)

KNUTSFORD Princess Street (Wesleyan Methodist: Macclesfield Circuit later Alderley Edge and Knutsford Circuit) f *c*1795 b 1864 (K 1928)
OR ZC 1801-37 (PRO: RG 4/183); C 1837-1942 (CRO)
Cop (Mf) ZC 1801-37 (CRO, SLC)

KNUTSFORD Brook Street (Independent) f 1826 (K 1928)
OR ZC 1806-37 (PRO: RG 4/172)
Cop (Mf) ZC 1806-37 (Ts I CRO, Manchester Local Hist Lib, SLC)

KNUTSFORD St Vincent de Paul, Tatton Street (Roman Catholic) f 1866 reb 1927 (K 1928)

KNUTSFORD Ollerton Chapel (Wesleyan Methodist) f 1886
OR C 1908-70, M 1958-72 (CRO)

LACH DENNIS All Saints (32) township in Great Budworth, created a parish in 1900
OR CMB 1896+ (Inc)

LACHE cum SALTNEY Holy Epiphany later St Mark created a parish in 1855 from Chester St Mary on the Hill and Hawarden, Flintshire
OR C 1853-1984, M 1857-1981, Banns 1963-82 (CRO)
BT 1873-84, 1888-98 (+ index C 1873-84, 1888-91) (CRO)

LACHE cum SALTNEY East Saltney (Wesleyan Methodist) b 1900, reb 1961
OR M 1954-61 (Chester RO)

LACHE cum SALTNEY East Saltney (Primitive Methodist) (K 1928)

LACHE cum SALTNEY East Saltney (Baptist) (K 1928)

LACHE cum SALTNEY St Anthony, East Saltney (Roman Catholic) (K 1928)

LACHE cum SALTNEY East Saltney (Presbyterian) (K 1928)

LACHE cum SALTNEY St Clare, Hawthorn Road (Roman Catholic) f 1960

LANCASHIRE QUAKER REGISTERS From 1802 to 1837 Runcorn, Great Budworth and Latchford (in Grappenhall) were in Lancashire Quarterly Meeting. From 1831 to 1837 Birkenhead, Southport Chester and Wallasey were also in Lancashire Quarterly Meeting.
OR (Lancashire Quarterly Meeting) Z 1796-1837, M 1795-1837, B 1799-1837 (PRO: RG 6/376, 639-642, 644-645, 1005, 1007-1008, 1041-1044, 1096, 1156) (Hardshaw West Monthly Meeting) Z 1798-1836, M 1798-1837, B 1798-1838 (PRO: RG 6/380, 528, 1529-1530, 1564)
Cop Z 1796-1837, M 1795-1837, B 1798-1837 (CRO, SLC)

LANDICAN township in Woodchurch (61)

LARKTON township in Malpas (44)

LATCHFORD St James, Wilderspool Causeway (2,166) chapelry in Grappenhall, created a parish in 1796 from Grappenhall, Thelwall and Warrington, Lancashire [Bucklow Hundred; Runcorn Union]
OR C 1777-1942, M 1833-1944, B 1782-1961 (CRO)
BT 1784-1841, 1851, 1882 (+ index C 1882) (CRO)
Cop M 1833-39 (CMI)
Cop (Mf) C 1777-1914, M 1833-1910, B 1782-1917 (CRO)

LATCHFORD Christ Church, Walsh Lane created a parish in 1866 from Grappenhall
OR C 1863-1902, M 1866-1940 (CRO)

LATCHFORD Meeting House (Society of Friends). From 1802 to 1837 Latchford was in Lancashire Quarterly Meeting.
OR see Cheshire Quaker Registers; Lancashire Quaker Registers

LATCHFORD Bethel Chapel, Acker's Lane (Baptist) b 1852 (K 1928)

LATCHFORD Our Lady of the Assumption, St Mary Street (Roman Catholic) b 1869 (K 1928)

LATCHFORD Knutsford Road (Wesleyan Methodist) b 1898 (K 1928)

LATCHFORD St John's, Wilderspool Causeway (Presbyterian) (K 1928)

LATCHFORD Knutsford Road (Primitive Methodist) (K 1928)

LATCHFORD Latchford Without (Independent Methodist) (K 1928)

LATCHFORD St Augustine of Canterbury and the English Martyrs, Henshall Avenue (Roman Catholic) f 1930

LAWTON, CHURCH All Saints (516) [Northwich Hundred; Congleton Union]
OR C 1559-1990, M 1559-1991, Banns 1754-1905, 1927-81, B 1559-1966 (CRO)
BT 1596, 1608, 1610-11, 1613-15, 1617-21, 1623-24, 1626-28, 1630, 1633-35, 1638-39, 1641, 1660, 1663-66, 1668-69, 1671-72, 1674-76, 1679-85, 1690-1704, 1708-17, 1720-83, 1785-1830, 1839, 1864-79 (+ index CB 1873-79) (CRO)
Cop M 1596-1830 (Ts CRO, SG); M 1693-1705, 1785-1837 (CMI); M 1596-1837 (NCMI)
Cop (Mf) C 1559-1990, M 1559-1924, B 1559-1913 (CRO)

LAWTON, CHURCH Hall Green (Wesleyan Methodist) b 1874 (K 1928)

LAWTON, MOOR St Michael and All Angels created a parish in 1937 from Northenden and Baguley
OR CM 1937+ (Inc)

LEA township in Wybunbury (56)

LEA by BACKFORD township in Backford (92)

LEA NEWBOLD township in Chester St Oswald (43)

LEASOWE St Chad created a parish in 1957 from Moreton, Great Meols, Bidston, Wallasey and Wallasey St Nicholas
OR CM 1957+ (Inc)

LEDSHAM township in Neston (70)

LEESE township in Sandbach (126)

LEFTWICH Farm of Good Shepherd township in Davenham (1,799)
OR C 1953-70 (CRO)

LEGH, HIGH St John (983) chapelry in Rostherne, created a parish in 1817 [Bucklow Hundred; Altrincham Union 1836-95, Bucklow Union 1895-1930]
OR C 1815-1956, M 1966-89 (CRO)
BT 1819, 1821-78, 1882-1902 (+ index C 1873-79, 1883-87) (CRO)

LEIGH, LITTLE St Michael and All Angels (381) chapelry in Great Budworth, created a parish in 1728 [Bucklow Hundred; Northwich Union]
OR C 1782-1937, M 1844-1983, Banns 1844-1956, B 1841-1915 (CRO)
BT 1813-45, 1847-56, 1858-64 (Ms CRO)
Cop 1782-1812 (CRO); M 1844-1900 (MCMI)
Cop (Mf) C 1782-1937, M 1844-47, B 1841-1915 (CRO); C 1782-1804 (SG)

LEIGH, LITTLE (Baptist) (K 1928)

LEIGH, LITTLE Bartington (Wesleyan Methodist) (K 1928)

LEIGHTON township in Neston (333)

LEIGHTON cum MINSHULL VERNON St Peter (261) township in Nantwich, created a parish in 1850
OR C 1840-1991, M 1861-1983, Banns 1861-1990, B 1840-1991 (CRO)
BT 1840-43, 1851, 1856-68 (CRO)

LEIGHTON cum MINSHULL VERNON Leighton Moor Chapel (Primitive Methodist) b 1841, closed 1899, congregation went to Bradfield Road, Crewe

LEIGHTON cum MINSHULL VERNON Cross Lanes, Bradfield Green (Independent)

LEIGHTON cum MINSHULL VERNON Bradfield Green (Wesleyan Methodist) (K 1928)

LINDOW St John the Evangelist created a parish in 1877 from Chorley
OR CMB 1877+ (Inc)
BT 1877-1903 (+ index CB 1877-91) (CRO)

LISCARD Wallasey Cemetery, Rake Lane (K 1946)

LISCARD St Mary (967) township in Wallasey, created a parish in 1878 from Wallasey
OR C 1877-1925, M 1878-1930 (CRO)

LISCARD St Columba, Trafalgar Avenue later Sea Bank Road, created a parish in 1922 from Egremont St John
OR C 1904-71, M 1922-71 (CRO)

LISCARD St Thomas the Apostle created a parish in 1925 from Liscard St Mary
OR C 1900-23, M 1929-35, Banns 1929-46 (CRO)

LISCARD St Alban, Mill Lane (Roman Catholic) f 1841

LISCARD Rake Lane (Independent, later United Reformed Church) b 1841, *fl.* 1991

LISCARD Meeting House, Withen's Lane (Society of Friends) f 1847, b 1854 (K 1924)
BT 1865-97 (CRO)

LISCARD Martins Lane (Welsh Independent) b 1888 (K 1924-46)

LISCARD Memorial Church, Manor Road (Unitarian) b 1888 (K 1924-46)

LISCARD Manor Road (Wesleyan Methodist: Wallasey Circuit) b 1893 (K 1946)

LISCARD Sea Bank Road (Baptist) f 1894 (K 1924)

LISCARD Serpentine Road (Welsh Methodist) b *c*1900, closed 1976
OR M 1925-70 (CRO)

LISCARD Christ Church, Martin's Lane (Free Church of England) b 1914 (K 1946)

LISCARD Martin's Lane (English Presbyterian) (K 1924)

LITTLE BUDWORTH *see* **BUDWORTH, LITTLE**

LITTLE LEIGH *see* **LEIGH, LITTLE**

LITTLETON township in Christleton (48)

LOSTOCK GRALAM St John the Evangelist (537) township in Great Budworth, created a parish in 1842 from Great Budworth and Witton
OR C 1844-1930, M 1863-1942, B 1863-1940 (CRO)
Cop M 1863-1900 (MCMI)
BT 1892 (CRO)

LOSTOCK GRALAM (Wesleyan Methodist) b 1894 (K 1928)

LOSTOCK GRALAM Lostock Green (Wesleyan Methodist) (K 1928)

LOW MARPLE *see* **MARPLE, LOW**

LOWER PEOVER *see* **PEOVER, LOWER**

LYME HANDLEY township in Prestbury (222)

LYMM St Mary the Virgin (2,305) [Bucklow Hundred; Altrincham Union 1836-95, Bucklow Union 1895-1930]
OR C 1568-1890, M 1568-1905, B 1568-1909 (CRO)
BT 1600, 1610, 1613, 1617-18, 1621-25, 1627-33, 1636-41, 1658-60, 1663, 1665-66, 1668-76, 1680-82, 1684-85, 1690-1703, 1706-39, 1741-50, 1752-1880 (+ index CB 1873-80) (CRO)
Cop M 1568-1812 (Ptd, Phil 1, 1909); M 1651-75, 1701-50, 1776-1812 (Boyd); M 1568-1837 (NCMI); M 1701-20, 1799-1837 (CMI)
Cop (Mf) C 1568-1890, M 1568-1905, B 1568-1909 (CRO, Manchester Local Hist Lib)

LYMM New Road (Wesleyan Methodist: Warrington Circuit) b 1809, reb 1879, closed 1968
OR ZC 1809-37 (PRO: RG 4/2151); M 1929-67 (CRO)
Cop ZC 1809-37 (Ptd, *Family History Society of Cheshire Journal* 8 (3), 1979)
Cop (Mf) ZC 1809-37 (CRO, SLC)

LYMM Cherry Lane (Baptist) b 1810 (K 1928)

LYMM Eagle Brow (Primitive Methodist) b 1849, reb 1897 (K 1928)
OR ZC 1837+ (Ch Sec)
Cop ZC 1837-62 (Ptd, M. Jackson, *Quarterly Journal of the Lymm and District Local History Society* 66 (2-3), 1983)

LYMM Cherry Lane (Independent Methodist) b 1849 (K 1928)

LYMM Higher Lane (Baptist) b 1850, *fl.* 1989

LYMM Brookfield Road (Independent, later United Reformed Church) b 1863, *fl.* 1991

LYMM St Winefride, Booth's Hill Road (Roman Catholic) f 1905

MACCLESFIELD Board of Guardians
OR ZCD 1848-1949 (Chester RO)

MACCLESFIELD Cemetery, Prestbury Road (opened 1866; 36 acres)

MACCLESFIELD St Michael and All Angels, Market Place (23,129) township in Prestbury until 1813
OR C 1572-1888, M 1572-1754, 1835-94, Banns 1835-1948, B 1572-1873 (CRO)
BT 1586, 1590, 1600, 1605, 1608, 1611, 1615, 1617-20, 1622-23, 1625-26, 1628-38, 1640-41, 1663-93, 1695-97, 1700-06, 1708-1845, 1884-85, 1889-92) (apart from 1722-54, marriages are entered on Prestbury BT) (CRO)
Cop 1572-1667 (Macclesfield Lib, Manchester Local Hist Lib); C 1572-1797, M 1573-1753 (Chester AS); C 1575-1665, M 1674-80, 1699-1754, B 1574-1667 (SG); M 1699-1754 (Ts CRO); M 1574-1655, 1664-83 (Ptd, Parish Magazine); M 1574-1754 (NCMI); M 1699-1709, 1730-54, 1790-1801 (CMI)
Cop (Mf) C 1572-1888, M 1572-1754, 1835-1894, B 1572-1873 (CRO, Macclesfield Lib, Manchester Local Hist Lib); C 1712-60, 1771-1812, M 1572-75, 1590-1630, 1699-1712, 1723-54, 1789-1810 (SG)

MACCLESFIELD Christ Church, Great King Street, created from St Michael, 1837
OR C 1773-1983, M 1889-1982, B 1773-1961 (CRO)
BT 1779-80, 1800-14, 1816-29 (1830-45 in St Michael series) (CRO)
Cop (Mf) C 1773-1943, M 1889-1948, B 1773-1961 (CRO); M 1793-1837 (SG)

MACCLESFIELD St Paul, Hallefield, created from St Michael, 1844
OR C 1844-1920, M 1844-1933, B 1844-1966 (CRO)
BT 1874-76, 1888 (and index CB 1874-76) (CRO)
Cop (Mf) C 1844-1920, M 1844-1914, B 1844-1966 (CRO)

MACCLESFIELD St Peter, Windmill Street, created from St Michael, 1844
OR C 1846-1919, M 1849-1937, B 1849-1947 (CRO)
BT 1874-76, 1895-96 (+ index C 1874-76) (CRO)

MACCLESFIELD St John the Evangelist created from St Michael, 1888
OR C 1873-1966, M 1888-1966, Banns 1888-1989 (CRO)
Cop (Mf) C 1873-1929, M 1888-1914 (CRO)

MACCLESFIELD Calemine Street later (1873) St George Street (Baptist) f 17th century, reb 1873, *fl.*1989

MACCLESFIELD Meeting House, Mill Street (Society of Friends) f 17th century disused by 1928 (K 1928)
<u>OR</u> see Cheshire Quaker Registers

MACCLESFIELD Back Street later King Edward Street (Unitarian) f 1672 b 1689, *fl.*1964
<u>OR</u> C 1713-1837 (PRO: RG 4/216, 2904, 3535); C 1840-1920 (CRO)
<u>Cop</u> (Mf) C 1713-1837 (CRO, SLC)

MACCLESFIELD Ebenezer Chapel, King Edward Street (1689) later (1787) Townley Street, Park Green (Independent) f 1689, reb 1787, 1877 (K 1928) now closed
<u>OR</u> ZC 1785-1837, B 1789-1835 (PRO: RG 4/539); C 1785-1920, M 1851-1920, B 1789-1879, 1881-1920 (CRO in two collections)
<u>Cop</u> (Mf) ZC 1785-1837, B 1789-1835 (CRO, Manchester Local Hist Lib, SLC)

MACCLESFIELD Sunderland Street (Wesleyan Methodist) b 1779, closed 1969
<u>OR</u> ZC 1810-37 (PRO: RG 4/541-542); C 1838-1969, M 1871-1968 (CRO)
<u>Cop</u> (Mf) ZC 1810-37 (CRO, SLC)

MACCLESFIELD Roe Street (Independent) f 1829
<u>OR</u> C 1785-1909, B 1789-1835 (CRO); ZC 1831-37 (PRO: RG 4/540)
<u>Cop</u> (Mf) ZC 1831-37 (CRO, Manchester Local Hist Lib, SLC)

MACCLESFIELD St Alban, Chester Road (Roman Catholic) f 1792, b 1838 (K 1928)

MACCLESFIELD Parsonage Street, later Park Street (United Methodist: Park Green Circuit) f 1814, b 1837, closed 1953
<u>OR</u> ZC 1815-37 (PRO: RG 4/184); C 1815-37, 1848-1949, M 1920-49, B 1837-69, 1888-1941 (CRO)
<u>Cop</u> (Mf) ZC 1815-37 (CRO, SLC)

MACCLESFIELD Brunswick Chapel, Bridge Street, Mill Land, Sutton (Wesleyan Methodist) b 1824, closed 1986
<u>OR</u> ZC 1828-37, B 1824-37 (PRO: RG 4/423, 552); C 1837-1966, M 1861-1983, B 1845-1959 (CRO)
<u>Cop</u> (Mf) ZC 1828-37, B 1824-37 (CRO, SLC)

MACCLESFIELD Langley Chapel (Wesleyan Methodist) b 1825, *fl.*1860

MACCLESFIELD Beech Lane (Primitive Methodist) b 1830, *fl.*1980
<u>OR</u> C 1823-1945 (Circuit) (CRO)

MACCLESFIELD Church Street West (United Methodist: Park Green Circuit) b 1842, closed 1960
<u>OR</u> C 1872-1960, M 1909-59 (CRO)

MACCLESFIELD Parsonage Street (Unitarian) f 1806, closed 1887

MACCLESFIELD Broken Cross (Wesleyan Methodist) f 1811, b 1880 (K 1928)

MACCLESFIELD Park Green (United Methodist: Park Green Circuit) b 1857, closed 1940
<u>OR</u> C 1856-1920, 1929-40, M 1904-39 (CRO)

MACCLESFIELD Mount Tabor Chapel, Tabor Street (United Methodist) b *c*1861, closed 1966
<u>OR</u> 1891-1953 (CRO)

MACCLESFIELD Higginbotham Street (Primitive Methodist) b 1873 (K 1928)

MACCLESFIELD Trinity Chapel, Cumberland Street (Wesleyan Methodist) b 1874, closed 1966
OR C 1875-1966, M 1876-1965 (CRO)

MACCLESFIELD Spiritualist Free Chapel, Cumberland Street b 1879 (K 1928)

MACCLESFIELD Fountain Street (Wesleyan Methodist) b 1893, closed 1960
OR C 1934-53 (CRO)

MACCLESFIELD Bourne Chapel, Byron Street, Sutton (Primitive Methodist) b 1844, reb 1905, closed 1960
OR C 1919-59, M 1906-60 (CRO)

MACCLESFIELD Milk Street (Salvation Army) (K 1928)

MACCLESFIELD Stamford Road School Chapel (Methodist) f 1938, closed 1984
OR C 1938-86, M 1939-84 (CRO)

MACCLESFIELD St Edward the Confessor, London Road (Roman Catholic) f 1939

MACCLESFIELD FOREST St Stephen alias FOREST CHAPEL (279) township in Prestbury, created a parish, 1737
OR C 1675-1929, M 1891-1968, B 1731-46, 1780-1971 (CRO)
BT 1812-26, 1829-37 (CRO)

MACEFEN township in Malpas (48)

MALPAS Cemetery (opened 1875; 2½ acres)

MALPAS St Oswald (5,127) [part Brox Hundred, Cheshire, part Maylor Hundred, Flintshire; Wrexham Union]
OR C 1561-1948, M 1561-1987, Banns 1754-66, 1822-1975, B 1561-1905 (CRO)
BT 1584, 1599-1603, 1609-11, 1613-15, 1617-18, 1622-28, 1630, 1633, 1635, 1637-40, 1662, 1664, 1666-77, 1679-85, 1687-91, 1693-98, 1700-1849, 1851-93 (CRO)
Cop 1561-1812 (Ts CRO); M 1812-37 (CMI)
Cop (Mf) C 1561-1948, M 1561-1927, B 1561-1905 (CRO, Manchester Local Hist Lib)

MALPAS St Chad created from St Oswald, 1824

MALPAS (Baptist) (Lewis 1831)

MALPAS High Street (Independent, later United Reformed Church) f 1815, *fl.* 1991
OR ZC 1819-37 (PRO: RG 4/185)
Cop (Mf) ZC 1819-37 (CRO, Manchester Local Hist Lib, SLC)

MALPAS Overton (Wesleyan Methodist) (Lewis 1831)

MALPAS (Wesleyan Methodist) b *c*1860, closed *c*1968
OR M 1935-68 (CRO)

MALPAS Cuddington Road (Primitive Methodist) b 1894 (K 1928)

MALPAS Hampton (Primitive Methodist) (K 1928)

MALPAS Wigland (Primitive Methodist) (K 1928)

MALPAS St Joseph (Roman Catholic) f 1946

MANLEY St John the Evangelist (331) mission church and township in Frodsham

MARBURY township in Great Budworth (26)

MARBURY St Michael (811) chapelry, created a parish in 1870 [part Nantwich Hundred, part in New Bradford Hundred, Shropshire; Nantwich Union 1837-53, Whitchurch Union 1853-1930]
OR C 1538-1943, M 1538-1952, Banns 1755-1911, B 1538-1944 (CRO)
BT 1578, 1586, 1593, 1600, 1607-10, 1612-14, 1621, 1625-27, 1629, 1632-34, 1636-39, 1659-60, 1663-66, 1668-85, 1690, 1692-1716, 1718-32, 1734-35, 1737-39, 1741-1833, 1835-39, 1841-47, 1849-51, 1853-54, 1875-82 (and index CB 1875-82) (CRO)
Cop 1538-1717 (Nantwich Lib); C 1813-22 (Ts Index CRO); M 1748-1837 (CMI)
Cop (Mf) C 1538-1943, M 1538-1952, B 1538-1944 (CRO)

MARBURY Norbury (Wesleyan Methodist) b 1834, closed 1975
OR M 1939-58 (CRO)

MARBURY Norbury (Independent) b 1868

MARLSTON cum LACHE township in Chester St Mary on the Hill (130)

MARPLE All Saints (2,678) chapel in Stockport, created a parish in 1738 [Macclesfield Hundred; Stockport Union]
OR C 1655-1910, M 1655-1754, 1838-1920, B 1655-1899 (CRO); Banns 1883-1907 (Inc)
BT 1715, 1717-46, 1748-57, 1759-84, 1786-1843 (CRO)
Cop M 1656-1754 (Ptd, Phil 1, 1909); M 1656-1750 (Boyd); C 1655-1855, M 1655-1885, B 1655-1839 (Ms CRO); M 1656-1754 (NCMI); M 1738-47 (CMI)
Cop (Mf) C 1655-1964, M 1655-1754, 1920-57, B 1655-1947 (CRO, Manchester Local Hist Lib)

MARPLE Marple Bridge (Independent) f 1662 (K 1928)
OR ZC 1761-1840, B 1791-1837 (PRO: RG 4/505, 943)
Cop (Mf) ZC 1761-1840, B 1791-1837 (CRO, Manchester Local Hist Lib, SLC)

MARPLE (Wesleyan Methodist) f 1803, reb 1876 (K 1928)
OR C 1804-40, B 1806-40 (PRO: RG 4/167)
Cop (Mf) C 1804-40, B 1806-40 (CRO, SLC)

MARPLE Market Street (Primitive Methodist) b 1829, reb 1869 (K 1928)

MARPLE (United Methodist) f 1836, b 1876 (K 1928)

MARPLE BRIDGE St Mary, Hollin's Lane (Roman Catholic) f 1859, reb 1945
OR C 1858-1942 (Nottingham Diocesan Archives)

MARPLE, LOW St Martin created 1870 from Marple
OR C 1870-1967 (CRO); M 1871+ (Inc)
BT 1871-90, 1892 (+ index CB 1873-90) (CRO)

MARSTON St Paul (465) township in Great Budworth, created 1875 from Great Budworth and Lostock Graham
OR C 1874-1965, M 1874-1964, Banns 1875-1917, B 1875-1931 (CRO)
Cop M 1875-1900 (MCMI)

MARTHALL All Saints (281) township in Rostherne created 1840 from Rostherne and Knutsford
OR CMB 1839+ (Inc)
BT 1839-81, 1885, 1887, 1889-92 (and index CB 1873-92) (CRO)
Cop C 1839-1947, M 1866-1946, B 1843-1947 (CRO)

MARTON St James and St Paul (354) chapelry in Prestbury created 1728 [Macclesfield Hundred; Macclesfield Union]
OR C 1563-1837, M 1563-1744, 1769, B 1563-1846 (CRO); M 1889+ (Inc)
BT 1622-23, 1625, 1630, 1636, 1639-41, 1663-85, 1687-97, 1704, 1706, 1711, 1714-67, 1769-88, 1791-1860, 1864-1913 (CRO)
Cop M 1563-1769 (Ptd, Phil 5, 1913); M 1563-1769 (Boyd); M 1563-1754 (NCMI); M 1726-54 (CMI)

MARTON township in Whitegate (711)

MATLEY township in Mottram (262)

MEOLS, GREAT St John the Baptist, Birkenhead Road (198) created from Hoylake, Moreton, West Kirby St Andrew and Frankby, 1937
OR CM 1913+ (Inc)

MEOLS, GREAT (Presbyterian) f 1902 (K 1924)

MEOLS, LITTLE township in West Kirby (126)

MERE township in Rosthern (552)

MICKLEHURST All Saints created 1962 from Millbrook, Cheshire and Mossley, Lancashire [Diocese of Manchester]
OR M 1900-1939 (CRO); CB 1900+ (Inc)

MIDDLETON GRANGE township and extra-parochial place adjacent to Runcorn, incorporated in Aston, 1861 (13) [Buckland Hundred]

MIDDLEWICH St Michael (4,785) [part Northwich Hundred, part Eddisbury Hundred; Northwich Union]
OR C 1613-1934, M 1613-1945, Banns 1759-93, 1804-08, 1816-72, 1918-42, 1949-70, B 1613-1909 (CRO)
BT 1588, 1600, 1604, 1607-09, 1611, 1614-15, 1617-21, 1623, 1625-26, *c*1627, 1632, 1634-36, 1639, 1662-65, 1668-76, 1679-85, 1690-94, 1695?, 1696-1877 (and index CB 1873-77) (CRO)
Cop 1613-1812 (Chester AS); M 1752-1837 (CMI)
Cop (Mf) C 1613-1905, M 1613-1919, B 1613-1909 (CRO, Winsford Lib); CB 1751-95, M 1751-1812 (SG)

MIDDLEWICH Queen Street (Independent, later United Reformed Church) f 1797, *fl.*1991
OR ZC 1807-37, B 1817-25 (PRO: RG 4/186)
Cop (Mf) ZC 1807-37, B 1817-25 (CRO, Manchester Local Hist Lib, SLC)

MIDDLEWICH Meeting House (Society of Friends) (Lewis 1831) but probably discontinued *c*1800
OR see Cheshire Quaker Registers

MIDDLEWICH Central Chapel, Lewin Street (Wesleyan Methodist) b 1828, reb 1909, closed 1969
OR C 1840-1940, M 1918-69 (CRO)

MIDDLEWICH Weaver Chapel (United Methodist) b 1840, *fl.*1976

MIDDLEWICH Lewin Street (Primitive Methodist) b 1841, reb 1963

MIDDLEWICH Sproston (Primitive Methodist) b 1845, closed 1940s

MIDDLEWICH Clive Green (United Methodist) b 1849 (K 1928)

MIDDLEWICH Chester Road, Newton by Middlewich (United Methodist) f 1863, b 1883, *fl.*1972
<u>OR</u> C 1868-1904 (CRO)

MIDDLEWICH St Mary, New King Street (Roman Catholic) f 1865, b 1891
<u>OR</u> C 1866-1953, M 1869-1942 (CRO)

MIDDLEWICH Occlestone (Primitive Methodist) b 1871, closed 1961

MILLBROOK St James created from Stalybridge St Paul, 1863
<u>OR</u> CMB 1863+ (Inc)
<u>BT</u> 1873-98 (and index CB 1873-77) (CRO)

MILLINGTON township in Rostherne (330)

MINSHULL, CHURCH St Bartholomew (468) chapelry in Acton until 1541 [Northwich Hundred; Nantwich Union]
<u>OR</u> C 1561-1849, M 1561-1837, B 1561-1874 (CRO)
<u>BT</u> 1605, 1607, 1609-12, 1614, 1616-18, 1621-24, 1626, 1629, 1637, 1641, 1658-64, 1666, 1668-85, 1687-89, 1691-97, 1699-1704, 1707-1870, 1884-94 (and index to CB 1884-93) (CRO)
<u>Cop</u> 1561-1851 (Ts Index, CRO); M 1561-1837 (NCMI); M 1791-1837 (CMI)
<u>Cop</u> (Mf) C 1561-1849, M 1561-1837, B 1561-1874 (CRO, Manchester Local Hist Lib)

MINSHULL, CHURCH (Independent) (Lewis 1831)

MINSHULL VERNON township in Middlewich (385)

MINSHULL VERNON (Independent, later United Reformed Church) f 1806, *fl.*1991
<u>OR</u> C 1809-24 (CRO)
<u>Cop</u> (Mf) C 1809-24 (CRO)

MINSHULL VERNON (Wesleyan Methodist) b 1830, closed 1952

MOBBERLEY St Wilfrid [Bucklow Hundred; Altrincham Union 1836-95; Bucklow Union 1895-1930]
<u>OR</u> C 1578-1898, M 1578-1933, Banns 1754-1812, B 1578-1838 (CRO)
<u>BT</u> 1599, 1608, 1610-11, 1615, 1617-19, 1621-22, 1624-26, 1628-29, 1631, 1635, 1640, 1664, 1666-78, 1680-85, 1690, 1706-29, 1731-1837, 1839-84 (and index CB 1873-84) (CRO)
<u>Cop</u> C 1578-1959, M 1578-1959, B 1578-1905 (CRO, Manchester Local Hist Lib); C 1578-1730, M 1578-1735, B 1579-1732 (Chester AS); M 1813-37 (NCMI); M 1731-1837 (CMI)
<u>Cop</u> (Mf) C 1578-1898, M 1578-1933, B 1578-1838 (CRO, Manchester Local Hist Lib)

MOBBERLEY Knolls Green (Independent) b 1783 for Wesleyans, taken over by Independents in 1803, closed 1961, registrations included in Brook Street, Knutsford

MOBBERLEY Pepper Street (Independent) (Lewis 1831) (K 1928)

MOBBERLEY Faulkner Lane (Wesleyan Methodist) f 1836, b 1882, *fl.*1965

MOBBERLEY Burial Ground (Society of Friends) (K 1928)
<u>OR</u> B 1655-1742 (PRO: RG 6/1603); see also Cheshire Quaker Registers
<u>Cop</u> B 1655-1742 (CRO, SLC)

MOLLINGTON BANASTRE township in Chester St Mary (24)

MOLLINGTON TARRANT township in Backford (118)

MOORE township in Runcorn (298)

MOORESBARROW cum PARME township in Middlewich (25)

MORETON Christ Church (247) township in Bidston b 1863
OR C 1863-1973, M 1864-1977, Banns 1864-1980 (CRO)
BT 1863-94 (CRO)

MORETON Sacred Heart, The Cross (Roman Catholic) f 1923

MORETON Our Lady of Lourdes, Leasowe Road (Roman Catholic) f 1957

MORETON township in Astbury (141)

MORETON cum ALCUMLOW township in Astbury

MORLEY Meeting House (Society of Friends) *see* Wilmslow

MOSSLEY Holy Trinity township in Astbury created parish, 1858
OR C 1845-86 (CRO); MB 1845+ (Inc)
BT 1857-58, 1871-91 (and index CB 1873-78) (CRO)

MOSTON township in Chester St Mary on the Hill (17)

MOSTON township in Warmingham (372)

MOTTRAM in LONGDENDALE Cemetery (2½ acres)

MOTTRAM in LONGDENDALE St Michael (15,536) [Macclesfield Hundred; Ashton under Lyne Union]
OR C 1562-1975, M 1559-1984, Banns 1830-55, 1950-88, B 1559-1988 (CRO)
BT 1583, 1586, 1590, 1595, 1599-1600, 1605, 1607-08, 1610, 1612, 1614-15, 1617-23, 1625, 1627-30, 1632-37, 1639-41, 1664-71, 1673-77, 1679-82, 1684-85, 1687, 1689-95, 1697-99, 1701-51, 1753, 1755-1835, 1837-38, 1884-92 (CRO)
Cop (Mf) C 1562-1975, M 1559-1949, B 1559-1988 (CRO); 1559-1838 (Tameside Lib); M 1770-1810 (SG)

MOTTRAM in LONGDENDALE Matley (United Methodist) f 1797 b 1909 (K 1928)
OR B 1798-1834 (PRO: RG 4/187)
Cop (Mf) B 1798-1834 (CRO, SLC)

MOTTRAM in LONGDENDALE Hyde (Independent) b 1830 (K 1928)

MOTTRAM in LONGDENDALE (Wesleyan Methodist) (Lewis 1831) (K 1928)

MOTTRAM in LONGDENDALE (Unitarian) b 1846 (K 1928)

MOTTRAM in LONGDENDALE The Immaculate Conception, Broadbottom (Roman Catholic) f 1896
OR C 1895-1954 (Nottingham Diocesan Archives)

MOTTRAM in LONGDENDALE St Andrew township in Prestbury (387)

MOULDSWORTH St Cuthbert (Roman Catholic) f 1955

MOULDSWORTH township in Tarvin (180)

MOULTON St Stephen the Martyr (243) township in Davenham, created 1877
OR C 1878-1973, M 1878-1983 (CRO)
Cop M 1878-1900 (MCMI)
BT 1878-1904 (and index C 1878-90) (CRO)

MOULTON Chapel Lane (Independent, later United Reformed Church) f 1833, *fl.*1991
OR B 1837-41 (CRO)

MOULTON (Primitive Methodist) b 1842, reb 1875 (K 1928)

MOW COP *see* **RODE, ODD**

NANTWICH Board of Guardians
OR Z 1872-1909 (CRO)

NANTWICH Cemetery (opened 1875; 3 acres)

NANTWICH St Mary and St Nicholas (5,357) chapelry in Acton, created a parish in 1677 [Nantwich Borough; Nantwich Union]
OR C 1539-1944, M 1539-1949, Banns 1917-37, B 1539-1943 (CRO)
BT 1596, 1602-03, 1605, 1607-14, 1617-18, 1620, 1622, 1624, 1626-30, 1632-33, 1636-39, 1658-85, 1687-1724, 1728-39, 1741-68, 1770-1894 (+ index CB 1873-93) (CRO)
Cop C 1573-1828, M 1572-1836, B 1572-1847 (Chester AS); C 1596-1639, M 1603-39, B 1607-39 (Chester City Lib); CMB 1539-1812 (Ts CRO); M 1645-89, 1700-1813, 1837 (CMI)
Cop (Mf) C 1539-1917, M 1539-1902, B 1539-1923 (CRO, Manchester Local Hist Lib)

NANTWICH Market Street (Baptist) f 1653, b 1873, *fl.*1989

NANTWICH Hospital Street (Unitarian) f 1672 b 1830 (K 1928)
OR ZC 1783-94, 1811-35, B 1821-35 (PRO: RG 4/168); C 1894-1908 and few to 1953, M 1896-98, 1923, 1925, DB 1893-1900, 1914, 1925 (CRO)
Cop (Mf) ZC 1783-94, 1811-35, B 1821-35 (CRO, SLC)

NANTWICH Meeting House, Pillory Street (Society of Friends) f end of 17th century; by 1928 Salvation Army
OR (Nantwich Monthly Meeting) Z 1776-93, M 1776-89, B 1776-94 (PRO: RG 6/156, 254-255); (Fraudley and Nantwich Monthly Meeting) Z 1795-1837, M 1802-37, B 1795-1837 (PRO: RG 6/182, 215-216); see also Cheshire Quaker Registers
Cop Z 1776-1837, M 1776-89, 1802-37, B 1776-1837 (CRO, SLC)

NANTWICH Barker Street (Unitarian Baptist later Baptist) f 1700
OR Z 1813-37 (PRO: RG 4/189)

NANTWICH Church Lane or Monk's Lane (Independent, later United Reformed Church) f 1780 b 1842, *fl.*1991
OR ZC 1800-35 (PRO: RG 4/188); C 1813-55, B 1800-1905 (CRO); C 1800-34 (Manchester Local Hist Lib)
Cop (Mf) ZC 1800-35 (CRO, SLC)

NANTWICH Hospital Street (Wesleyan Methodist) b 1808 (K 1928)
OR ZC 1819-37 (PRO: RG 4/410)
Cop (Mf) ZC 1819-37 (CRO, SLC)

NANTWICH Welsh Row (Primitive Methodist) (Lewis 1831) b 1840, *fl.*1950

NANTWICH St Anne, Pillory Street, off Welsh Row (Roman Catholic) f 1856, reb 1860
OR C 1868-1963, M 1869, 1939, DB 1868-1966 (CRO)

NANTWICH Ebenezer Chapel, Castle Street (United Methodist) b 1857, closed 1908, replaced by Pillory Street

NANTWICH Willaston (Wesleyan Methodist) b 1864

NANTWICH Broad Lane (Primitive Methodist) b 1864

NANTWICH Woolstanwood (Wesleyan Methodist) b 1870, closed 1969

NANTWICH Willaston (Primitive Methodist) b 1876, closed 1962
OR M 1928-62 (CRO)

NANTWICH Memorial Chapel, Barony (Primitive Methodist) b 1881, closed 1965
OR M 1920-65 (CRO)

NANTWICH Pillory Street (United Methodist) b 1908, closed 1966
OR M 1913-65 (CRO)

NANTWICH Pillory Street (Salvation Army) (K 1928)

NESS township in Neston (480)

NESTON Cemetery (opened 1905; 2½ acres)

NESTON St Mary and St Helen (3,518) [Wirral Hundred; Wirral Union]
OR C 1559-1965, M 1559-1974, Banns 1754-1809, 1823-1989, B 1559-1918 (CRO)
BT 1581, 1587, 1593, 1603?, 1605, 1607, 1609-10, 1612, 1617-24, 1626-27, 1630, 1632, 1634, 1636, 1638-39, 1641-42, 1666-70, 1672-77, 1679-85, 1694-95, 1700-42, 1744-45, 1747-1838, 1871-74 (+ index CB 1873-74) (CRO)
Cop 1561-1671 (Chester City Lib); C 1700-34 (Ts I CRO); M 1701-33, 1800-37 (CMI)
Cop (Mf) C 1559-1901, M 1559-1911, B 1559-1918 (CRO, Manchester Local Hist Lib); C 1829-1901, M 1754-1837 (Neston Lib)

NESTON Park Street and High Street (Wesleyan Methodist) (Lewis 1831) b 1908, *fl.* 1966

NESTON St Winefride, Burton Road, Little Neston (Roman Catholic) b 1843 (K 1928)

NESTON (Independent, later United Reformed Church) f 1857 b 1909, *fl.* 1991

NESTON Zion Chapel, Little Neston (Primitive Methodist) b 1872, *fl.* 1973

NESTON (Presbyterian) b 1884 (K 1928)

NESTON Chapel (Wesleyan Methodist: Bebington South Circuit) (K 1924-46)

NETHERPOOL township in Eastham (19)

NEWALL GREEN St Francis created a parish in 1960 from Northenden
OR CM 1960+ (Inc)

NEWBOLD ASTBURY township in Astbury (598)

NEW FERRY St Mark the Evangelist, New Chester Road created a parish in 1888 from Nether Bebington
OR C 1866-1948, M 1889-1949 (CRO)
Cop (Mf) C 1866-1902, M 1889-1912 (CRO)

NEW FERRY Chapel, Bebington Road (Wesleyan Methodist: Bebington South Circuit)
b 1891, closed 1963
OR C 1876-1921, M 1893-1963 (CRO)

NEW FERRY Beaconsfield Road b 1913, reb 1966 as **Trinity Methodist Church**
(Primitive Methodist: Second Circuit)
OR C 1917-62, M 1970-89 (CRO)

NEWHALL township in Audlem (1,011)

NEWHALL township in Davenham (22)

NEWTON township in Middlewich (1,649)

NEWTON township in Prestbury (90)

NEWTON by CHESTER township in Chester St Oswald (213)

NEWTON by DARESBURY township in Runcorn (165)

NEWTON by FRODSHAM township in Frodsham (130)

NEWTON by MALPAS township in Malpas (17)

NEWTON by TATTENHALL township in Tattenhall (67)

NEWTON in MOTTRAM St Mary (5,997) township in Mottram, created a parish in 1840
OR C 1839-1960, M 1842-1991, Banns 1852-82, 1955-85, B 1839-1960 (CRO)
BT 1839-72 (CRO)

NEWTON St Stephen, Flowery Field created a parish in 1891 from Newton in Mottram
OR C 1891-1938, M 1891-1962 (CRO)

NEWTON with LARTON township in West Kirby (56)
OR CM 1915+ (Inc)

NOCTORUM township in Woodchurch (28)

NORBURY St Thomas chapelry in Stockport, created a parish in 1737
[Macclesfield Hundred; Stockport Union]
OR C 1829-1953, M 1837-1956, B 1834-98 (CRO)
BT 1829-77 (+ index CB 1873-77) (CRO)
Cop (Mf) C 1829-1905, M 1837-1913, B 1834-98 (CRO, Manchester Local Hist Lib)

NORBURY Ebenezer Chapel, Hazel Grove (Independent) b 1827 (K 1928)
OR ZC 1827-37, B 1828-37 (PRO: RG 4/182, 1103)
Cop (Mf) ZC 1827-37, B 1828-37 (CRO, SLC)

NORBURY Commercial Road (Primitive Methodist) b 1849 reb 1896 in London Road
(K 1928)

NORBURY Hazel Grove (Independent Methodist) b 1856, reb 1877 (K 1928)

NORBURY Hazel Grove (United Methodist) b 1877 (K 1928)

NORBURY Hazel Grove (Wesleyan Methodist) b 1885 (K 1928)

NORBURY Offerton (Wesleyan Methodist) b 1887 (K 1928)

NORBURY St Peter, Commercial Road or Green Lane, Hazel Grove (Roman Catholic) f 1897 (K 1928)

NORLEY St John the Evangelist (502) chapelry in Frodsham, created a parish in 1861
OR CMB 1855+ (Inc)
Cop M 1838-1900 (MCMI)
BT 1855-56, 1887-99 (+ index CB 1891) (CRO)

NORLEY Central Chapel (Wesleyan Methodist) f 1779, reb 1882 (K 1928)
OR C 1871-91 (CRO)

NORLEY Bethel Chapel (United Methodist) b 1836
OR C 1909-68 (CRO)

NORLEY (Primitive Methodist) (K 1928)

NORLEY Our Lady of the Assumption, Wickentree, Blakemore Lane, Hatchmere (Roman Catholic) f 1945, closed 1982
OR M 1981-82 (CRO)

NORTHENDEN St Wilfrid (1,420) [Macclesfield Hundred; Altrincham Union 1836-95, Bucklow Union 1895-1930]
OR CMB 1563+ (Inc)
BT 1608, 1611, 1619-24, 1627-29, 1631-37, 1639-41, 1663, 1665-84, 1708-1877 (+ index CB 1873-77) (CRO)
Cop 1563-1680 (Ms I Chester AS, CRO); 1563-1781 (Manchester Local Hist Lib); M 1563-1837 (NCMI); M 1756-1819 (CMI)
Cop (Mf) C 1563-1852, M 1563-1837, B 1563-1853 (CRO)

NORTHENDEN (Wesleyan Methodist) b 1828 (White 1860)

NORTH RODE *see* **RODE, NORTH**

NORTHWICH Board of Guardians
OR Z 1849-1913, D 1855-1914 (CRO)

NORTHWICH Cemetery, Church Road (opened 1890)

NORTHWICH St Helen alias **WITTON St Helen** (1,481) township and parochial chapelry in Great Budworth [Northwich Hundred; Northwich Union]
OR C 1561-1958. M 1561-1961, Banns 1754-67, 1783-86, 1865-68, B 1561-1973 (CRO)
BT 1597, 1600, 1603, 1616-19, 1621-25, 1628-30, 1632-37, 1640-41, 1658-66, 1668-76, 1679-85, 1690-1717, 1719-39, 1741-1861, B 1886-87, CB 1888, B 1889-90, CB 1891-92, C 1893, CB 1897 (CRO)
Cop C 1754-92 (Ptd, Index, K. Musgrave and A. Moilliet, Family History Society of Cheshire, Northwich Group, 1986); M 1792-1851 (Ptd, Index, K. Musgrave and A. Moilliet, Family History Society of Cheshire, Northwich Group, 1986); C 1813-51 (Ptd, Index, K. Musgrave and A. Moilliet, Family History Society of Cheshire, Northwich Group, 1987); C 1792-1851 (Index, FHS of Cheshire); M 1700-1900 (MCMI); M 1754-1837 (NCMI); M 1604, 1668, 1751-1837 (CMI)
Cop (Mf) C 1561-1903. M 1561-1895, B 1561-1912 (CRO, Northwich Lib, Manchester Local Hist Lib)

NORTHWICH Holy Trinity, Castle Northwich, created a parish in 1929 from the township of Castle Northwich in Witton and Hartford
OR C 1842-1909 (CRO); M 1929+ (Inc)
Cop C 1842-1909 (CRO)

NORTHWICH St Luke, Winnington, created a parish in 1931 from Witton
OR CM 1884+ (Inc)

NORTHWICH Chapel or Leftwich Chapel, Witton Street (Wesleyan Methodist: Northwich Circuit) f 1777, reb 1889, closed 1964
OR ZC 1811-37 (PRO: RG 4/538); C 1839-1964 (Circuit), M 1902-69 (CRO)
Cop (Mf) ZC 1811-37 (CRO, SLC)

NORTHWICH Castle Street (Independent, later United Reformed Church) f 1708 b 1882, *fl.*1991
OR ZC 1800-37 (PRO: RG 4/2094)
Cop (Mf) ZC 1800-37 (CRO, Manchester Local Hist Lib, SLC)

NORTHWICH Central Chapel, Witton Street (United Methodist) f 1835, b 1854, closed 1954
OR C 1837-1935, 1944, M 1939-53 (CRO)

NORTHWICH St Wilfrid, Witton Street (Roman Catholic) f 1840, b 1866 (K 1928)
OR C 1857-1945, M 1856-1947, B 1862-1937 (CRO)

NORTHWICH Bourne Chapel, Witton Street (Primitive Methodist) f *c*1848, b 1877, closed *c*1970

NORTHWICH Ebenezer Chapel, Chapel Street, Castle (Wesleyan Methodist) b 1864, reb 1972
OR C 1889-1946 (CRO)

NORTHWICH Zion Street, Castle (Primitive Methodist) b 1864 (K 1928)

NORTHWICH Middlewich Road (United Methodist) b 1881, closed 1970
OR M 1954-69 (CRO)

NORTHWICH Station Road (Wesleyan Methodist) b 1881, closed 1977
OR C 1880-1973, M 1909-70 (CRO)

NORTHWICH Emmanuel (Evangelical)
OR C 1929+, M 1910+ (Ch Sec)
Cop C 1929-78, M 1910-79 (Ptd, K.A. Frobisher, 1982)

NORTHWICH Tabley Street (Salvation Army) (K 1928)

NORTHWICH Winnington Lane (Primitive Methodist) (K 1928)

NORTHWICH, CASTLE township in Great Budworth

NORTON St Berteline (306) township in Runcorn

OAKMERE township in Delamere (140)

OCCLESTONE township in Middlewich (93)

ODD RODE see **RODE, ODD**

OFFERTON St John township in Stockport

OLDCASTLE township in Malpas (98)

OLLERTON township in Knutsford (283)

ONSTON township in Weaverham (92)

ORFORD St Andrew and ORFORD St Margaret and All Hallows chapelries in Lancashire, transferred to Cheshire, 1974

OUGHTRINGTON St Peter created a parish in 1881 from Lymm
OR C 1872-1966, M 1882-1978, B 1872-1910 (CRO)
BT 1872-76, 1892-99, 1901 (+ index CB 1873-76) (CRO)

OULTON, LOW township in Over (55)

OVER St Chad [part Over Borough, part Eddisbury Hundred; Winsford Union]
OR C 1558-1911, M 1558-1912, Banns 1754-1812, B 1558-1917 (CRO)
BT 1588?, 1600, 1607-09, 1610?, 1613-15, 1617-20, 1623-30, 1633-37, 1641, 1658-66, 1668-76, 1679-85, 1687-89, 1696-1744, 1746-57, 1759-60, 1762, 1766-79, 1781-1876 (+ index CB 1873-76) (CRO)
Cop 1558-1739, M 1638-1722, B 1709-33 (Chester AS); C 1770-1812 (Ts Index CRO); M 1700-1900 (MCMI); M 1701-1837 (CMI)
Cop (Mf) C 1558-1911, M 1558-1912, B 1558-1917 (CRO, Winsford Lib, Manchester Local Hist Lib); C 1700-1812 (SG)

OVER St John the Evangelist created a parish in 1863 from St Chad and Whitegate
OR C 1863-1928, M 1863-1948, B 1868-1938 (CRO)

OVER (Independent) f 1814
OR With Ch Sec
Cop M 1886-89 (MCMI)

OVER Swanlow Lane (Wesleyan Methodist) b 1861, closed 1954
OR M 1925-49 (CRO)

OVER High Street (Wesleyan Methodist) b 1883, closed 1977
OR C 1887-1977, M 1904-76, Graves 1893-1901 (CRO)

OVERCHURCH (alias UPTON by BIRKENHEAD) St Mary (191) [Wirral Hundred; Wirral Union]
OR C 1759-1936, M 1755-1800, 1814-1941, B 1759-1937 (CRO)
BT 1600, 1609-10, 1613, 1615, 1617-25, 1633-34, 1636, 1668-71, 1675-76, 1680-82, 1684, 1691, 1694, 1699-1702, 1711, 1714, 1716, 1719-39, 1741-44, 1746, 1748-56, 1758-88, 1794-1813, 1825-31, 1833-38, 1848-49, 1851, 1868-92 (CRO)
Cop 1600-1812 (BT & OR) (Ptd, W.F. Irvine, PRS 33, 1900); CMB 1619 (BT missed in earlier work) (Ptd, *Cheshire Sheaf* 3rd series 6, 1907); M 1756-1838 (CMI)
Cop (Mf) C 1759-1936, M 1755-1800, 1814-1941, B 1759-1937 (CRO, Manchester Local Hist Lib)

OVERCHURCH St Joseph, Upton (Roman Catholic) f 1863

OVERCHURCH Ford Road (Independent, later United Reformed Church) b 1900, *fl.*1991

OVER PEOVER *see* **PEOVER, OVER**

OVERPOOL township in Eastham (93)

OVER TABLEY *see* **TABLEY, OVER**

OVERTON township in Malpas (111)

OXTON St Saviour (234) township in Woodchurch, created a parish in 1865 [Wirral Hundred; Wirral Union 1836-91, Birkinhead Union 1891-1930]
OR CMB 1851+ (Inc)
BT 1851-54, 1876-96 (+ index C 1873-91) (CRO)

For Nonconformist chapels *see* **BIRKENHEAD**

PADGATE Christ Church chapelry in Lancashire, transferred to Cheshire, 1974

PARKGATE St Thomas (created from Neston, 1976)
OR CM 1976+ (Inc)

PARTINGTON St Mary township in Bowdon, created a parish in 1885 from Carrington
OR CMB 1884+ (Inc)
BT 1891-1910 (+ index C 1886-89, CB 1890-91) (CRO)

PARTINGTON (Independent) f 1714, closed 1951
OR ZC 1815-37 (PRO: RG 4/93); C 1820-37 (Manchester Local Hist Lib)
Cop (Mf) ZC 1815-37 (CRO, SLC)

PARTINGTON (Wesleyan Methodist) b 1843, reb 1861 (K 1928)

PARTINGTON Our Lady of Lourdes, Chapel Lane (Roman Catholic) f 1957

PECKFORTON township in Bunbury (331)

PENKETH St Paul chapelry in Lancashire, transferred to Cheshire, 1974
see Lancashire NIPR

PENSBY St Michael and All Angels (22) township in Woodchurch
OR CM 1958+ (Inc)

PEOVER, LOWER St Oswald (226) township in Great Budworth, created a parish in 1814
OR C 1570-1896, M 1570-1974, Banns 1934-69, B 1570-1895 (CRO)
BT 1600, 1605, 1607-08, 1611, 1614, 1616-18, 1621-23, 1625, 1627-30, 1636-37, 1639-40, 1658-59, 1663, 1666-69, 1671-76, 1680, 1682-85, 1691-1703, 1707-08, 1711, 1713-39, 1741-1814, 1816-17, 1819, 1851, 1877-99 (+ index CB 1877-89) (CRO)
Cop C 1570-1843, M 1570-1836, B 1570-1843 (CRO); M 1754-1837 (NCMI); M 1700-17, 1747-1837 (CMI)
Cop (Mf) C 1570-1896, M 1570-1934, B 1570-1895 (CRO, Manchester Local Hist Lib); C 1628-30, M 1576-79, 1628-29, 1661-68, 1744-1836, B 1628-29 (SG)

PEOVER, LOWER Allostock (Unitarian) b 1689 (K 1928)

PEOVER, LOWER Bradshaw Brook (Wesleyan Methodist) b 1858 (K 1928)

PEOVER, LOWER Plumbley (Wesleyan Methodist) b 1887 (K 1928)

PEOVER, OVER St Laurence (561) township in Rostherne, created a parish in 1827
OR C 1664-1919, M 1664-1954, Banns 1754-1807, 1823, 1846-1901, B 1664-1956 (CRO)
BT 1600, 1614-16, 1621, 1624-25, 1631?, 1634-37, 1662-63, 1665-66, 1668-76, 1678-85, 1690-1827, 1829-46, 1848-82, 1905-07, 1910-11 (+ index CB 1873-82) (CRO)
Cop 1664-1812 (Chester AS, CRO); M 1754-1837 (NCMI); M 1669-78, 1710-23, 1754-1837 (CMI)
Cop (Mf) C 1664-1919, M 1664-1954, B 1664-1956 (CRO, Manchester Local Hist Lib)

PEOVER, OVER (United Methodist) b 1913 (K 1928)

PICKMERE township in Great Budworth (228)

PICTON township in Plemstall (97)

PLEMSTALL St Peter (737) [part Broxton Hundred, part Eddisbury Hundred; Great Boughton Union 1837-71, Chester Union 1871-1930]
OR C 1558-1909, M 1558-1949, Banns 1754-1812, 1824-1913, B 1558-1917 (CRO)
BT 1586, 1596, 1599-1600, 1605, 1607-08, 1610, 1614, 1617-18, 1623, 1627-35, 1637, 1640-41, 1666-72, 1674-77, 1679-84, 1702-19, 1721-90, 1792-1841, 1843-79 (+ index CB 1873-79) (CRO)
Cop M 1742-1837 (CMI)
Cop (Mf) C 1558-1909, M 1558-1949, B 1558-1917 (CRO, Manchester Local Hist Lib)

PLEMSTALL (Primitive Methodist) b 1885 (K 1928)

PLUMLEY township in Great Budworth (378)

POOLE township in Acton (188)

PORTWOOD St Paul, Great Portwood Street created a parish in 1844 from Brinnington township in Stockport, united to Brinnington, 1971
OR C 1851-1971, M 1851-1970, B 1851-1970 (CRO)
Cop M 1866-1970 (SG)
Cop (Mf) C 1851-1971, M 1851-1970, B 1851-1970 (CRO)

POTT SHRIGLEY St Christopher chapelry in Prestbury, created a parish in 1719 [Macclesfield Hundred; Macclesfield Union]
OR C 1630-1991, M 1630-1751, 1880-1969, B 1630-1881 (CRO)
BT 1679-80, 1692, 1696, 1732-1829, 1831-32, 1851 (CRO)
Cop M 1685-1751 (Ptd, Phil 5, 1913); C 1630-1754, M 1691-1710, B 1693-1811 (Chester AS); M 1685-1751 (Boyd); M 1685-1754 (NCMI); M 1709-52 (CMI)
Cop (Mf) C 1630-1883, M 1630-1751, B 1630-1881 (CRO, Manchester Local Hist Lib)

POTT SHRIGLEY Green Close (United Methodist) b 1861 (K 1928)

POULTON St Luke, Breck Road (1,212) created a parish in 1907 from Wallasey
OR CM 1900+ (Inc)

POULTON (Primitive Methodist: Second Circuit) (K 1924)

POULTON Oxton Road (Wesleyan Methodist: Wallasey Circuit) (K 1924-46)

POULTON township in Pulford (128)

POULTON cum SPITAL township in Bebington (120)

POULTON LANCELYN Holy Trinity
OR CM 1976+ (Inc)

POWNALL FEE township in Wilmslow (1,747)

POYNTON St George (747) chapelry in Prestbury, created a parish in 1745 [Macclesfield Hundred; Macclesfield Union]
OR C 1723-1988, M 1723-53, 1859-1994, Banns 1859-1979, B 1840-1922 (CRO)
BT 1723-27, 1729-98, 1800-02, 1804-05, 1807-27, 1829-63 (CRO)
Cop M 1723-53 (Ptd, Phil 5, 1913); M 1723-53 (Boyd, CMI, NCMI)
Cop (Mf) C 1723-1958, M 1723-1922, B 1840-1922 (CRO)

POYNTON (United Methodist) b 1845 (K 1928)

POYNTON (Primitive Methodist) b 1846 (K 1928)

POYNTON Park Lane (Baptist) b 1867, *fl.* 1989

POYNTON St Paul, Clumber Road (Roman Catholic) f 1941

PRENTON St Stephen (104) township in Woodchurch, created a parish in 1902 from Woodchurch, Tranmere St Paul and Oxton
OR C 1894-1954, M 1902-57 (CRO)

PRENTON Storeton Road (Independent) f 1909 (K 1946)

PRESTBURY St Peter (47,257) [Macclesfield Hundred; Macclesfield Union]
OR C 1560-1854, M 1560-1851, B 1560-1858 (CRO)
BT 1586, 1596, 1600, 1608, 1610, 1612, 1615, 1617, 1619-37, 1639-41, 1663-66, 1668-84, 1688-91, 1694-1738, 1740-44, 1747-1840, 1855-58 (CRO)
Cop 1560-1636 (Ptd, Lancs and Ches RS 5, J. Croston, 1881); M 1637-1789 (Ptd, Phil 2-4, 1910-12); 1560-1845 (Chester AS); 1637-85 (Liverpool Ref Lib); M 1560-1836 (CRO); M 156-1789 (Ts Index CRO); CB 1637-85, M 1637-1812 (SG); M 1626-1812 (Boyd); M 1560-1820, 1826-31 (NCMI); M 1790-1812 (CMI)
Cop (Mf) C 1560-1854, M 1560-1851, B 1560-1858 (CRO, Macclesfield Lib, Manchester Local Hist Lib); C 1748-73, 1777-1803, M 1789-1812, Banns 1755-66 (SG)

PRESTBURY Lower Withington (Wesleyan Methodist) b 1808, *fl.* 1961
OR ZC 1808-37 (PRO: RG 4/553)
Cop (Mf) ZC 1808-37 (CRO, SLC)

PRESTBURY Kettleshulme (Wesleyan Methodist: Buxton Circuit) f 1815
OR ZC 1808-36 (PRO: RG 4/2092)
Cop (Mf) ZC 1808-36 (CRO, SLC)

PRESTBURY Lower Withington (Primitive Methodist) b 1847, closed 1953

PRESTBURY Adlington (United Methodist) b 1870, closed 1957
OR M 1941-54 (CRO)

PRESTBURY Mottram St Andrew (Wesleyan Methodist) b 1895, *fl.* 1981

PRESTBURY Adlington (Wesleyan Methodist) (K 1928)

PRESTON BROOK St Faith mission church in Daresbury

PRESTON on the HILL township in Runcorn, later Daresbury (461)

PRIOR'S HEYS extra-parochial place until 1964, when incorporated in Tarvin

PUDDINGTON township in Burton (145)

PUDDINGTON (Wesleyan Methodist: Bebington South Circuit) f 1896 (K 1946)

PULFORD St Mary (289) united to Eccleston, 1973 [Broxton Hundred; Great Boughton Union 1837-53, Hawarden 1853-71, Chester Union 1871-1930]
OR C 1559-1884, M 1559-1836, Banns 1755-1812, 1876-1972, B 1559-1956 (CRO)
BT 1599-1601, 1603-06, 1608, 1610-11, 1613-18, 1622-25, 1627-36, 1640-41, 1666, 1668-70, 1672-73, 1675-77, 1679-84, 1686, 1690-92, 1694-96, 1703-04, 1709-11, 1713, 1715-21, 1723-28, 1731-1804, 1806-56, 1859-98, 1905, 1907, 1909-10 (+ index CB 1873-90) (CRO)
Cop 1599-1680 (Chester AS); 1681-1797 (Chester City Lib); M 1756-1837 (CMI)
Cop (Mf) C 1559-1884, M 1559-1836, B 1559-1956 (CRO, Manchester Local Hist Lib)

RABY township in Neston (165)

RADNOR township in Astbury (20)

RAINOW Holy Trinity (1,807) chapelry in Prestbury, created a parish in 1785, united to Macclesfield Forest, 1973
OR C 1765-1840, M 1846-1941, B 1815-95 (CRO)
BT 1765-87, 1793-1840, 1846-94 (+ index CB 1873-92) (CRO)
Cop C 1786-93 (Ts CRO)
Cop (Mf) C 1765-1840, M 1846-1941, B 1815-95 (CRO, Macclesfield Lib, Manchester Local Hist Lib)

RAINOW (Wesleyan Methodist) f 1807 b 1878
OR ZC 1808-36, B 1826-37 (PRO: RG 4/191, 544); M 1912-75 (CRO)
Cop (Mf) ZC 1808-36, B 1826-37 (CRO, SLC)

RAVENSCROFT township in Middlewich (16)

RIDLEY township in Bunbury (100)

RINGWAY St Mary and All Saints created a parish in 1722 from Bowdon
OR C 1783-1905, M 1864-1967 (CRO); B *c*1840+ (Inc)
BT 1786-98, 1800-16, 1818-92 (+ index CB 1873-91) (CRO)

ROCK FERRY Bebington Cemetery, Town Lane (K 1946)

ROCK FERRY St Peter, St Peter's Road, created a parish in 1844 from Higher Bebington
OR C 1844-1975, M 1844-1941, B 1844-1961 (CRO)
Cop (Mf) C 1844-1924, M 1844-1901 (CRO)

ROCK FERRY St Barnabas, Bedford Place, Rock Ferry, daughter church to St Peter
OR C 1895-1978, M 1941-78 (CRO)
Cop (Mf) C 1895-1903 (CRO)

ROCK FERRY New Chester Road (Presbyterian) b 1858 (K 1946)

ROCK FERRY Trinity Chapel, New Chester Road (Wesleyan Methodist: Bebington South Circuit) b 1866, closed 1963
OR C 1859-1963, M 1867-1963 (CRO)

ROCK FERRY Highfield Chapel, Rock Lane West (Independent, later United Reformed Church) b 1869, *fl.*1991

ROCK FERRY New Chester Road (Welsh Presbyterian) f 1870 (K 1924)

ROCK FERRY Blucher Hall later (1922) **Wesley Hall**, Blucher Street and Earl Street (Wesleyan Methodist) b 1889, closed 1954
OR C 1894-1953 (CRO)

ROCK FERRY New Chester Road (Baptist) f 1914, *fl.*1989

RODE, NORTH St Michael (256) township in Prestbury, created a parish in 1846
OR CMB 1846+ (Inc)
BT 1846-61, 1879-89 (+ index CB 1873-84) (CRO)

RODE, ODD All Saints (1,300) township in Astbury, created a parish in 1860
OR C 1809-16, 1851-1903, M 1865-1952 (CRO); Banns 1864+, B 1851+ (Inc)
BT 1864-84 (+ index CB 1873-84) (CRO)

RODE, ODD St Luke (Mow Cop)
OR CMB 1876+ (Inc)
BT index CB 1876-84 (CRO)

RODE, ODD Mow Cop Chapel (Primitive Methodist) b 1841, reb 1883, closed 1964

RODE, ODD Kent Green Chapel (Primitive Methodist) f 1873, b 1892 (K 1928)

RODE, ODD Hall Green, Lawton (Wesleyan Methodist) b 1874 (K 1928)

RODE, ODD Thurlwood Chapel (Primitive Methodist) b 1880s, closed 1963

RODE, ODD Bank (Wesleyan Methodist) (K 1928)

RODE, ODD Mount Pleasant Chapel (Wesleyan Methodist) (K 1928)

ROMILEY *see* **CHADKIRK**

ROPE township in Wybunbury (119)

ROSTHERNE St Mary (3,730) united to Bollington, 1973 [part Bucklow Hundred, part Macclesfield Hundred; Altrincham Union 1836-95, Bucklow Union 1895-1930]
OR C 1594-1919, M 1594-1870, Banns 1754-70, B 1594-1874 (CRO)
BT 1600, 1608?, 1612-13, 1616, 1621-23, 1627, 1631-33, 1635-40, 1658-61, 1663, 1665-66, 1668-76, 1678-85, 1690-96, 1698-1738, 1741-99, 1801, 1803-49, 1851-75 (+ index CB 1873, C 1874, CB 1875, CB 1876-86) (CRO)
Cop 1594-1812 (Chester AS); C 1595-1812, M 1603-1812, B 1603-1812 (Manchester Local Hist Lib); C 1595-1736, M 1595-1736, B 1595-1736 (John Rylands Lib, Manchester, SG); M 1594-1734, 1813-37 (NCMI); M 1754-61, 1801-37 (CMI)
Cop (Mf) C 1594-1919, M 1594-1870, B 1594-1874 (CRO, Manchester Local Hist Lib)

ROSTHERNE Snelson (Wesleyan Methodist) b 1825, *fl.*1964

ROSTHERNE (Independent) (K 1928)

ROWTON township in Christleton (122)

RUDHEATH township part in Davenham, part in Sandbach (367)
OR C 1931-67 (CRO)

RUNCORN Board of Guardians
OR Vaccinations 1871-1948 (CRO)

RUNCORN Cemetery, Greenway Road (opened 1857; 13 acres)

RUNCORN All Saints (10,326) [part Halton Borough, part Bucklow Hundred; Runcorn Union]
OR C 1558-1984, M 1558-1963, Banns 1955-86, B 1558-1936 (CRO)
BT 1581, 1584, 1600, 1607-08, 1610-12, 1614-18, 1621-25, 1627-30, 1633-41, 1659-60, 1663, 1665-66, 1668-76, 1678-85, 1687-1739, 1741-1853 (CRO)
Cop 1558-1812 (Ts I CRO); M 1681-85, 1770-74, 1813-37 (CMI)
Cop (Mf) C 1660-1907, M 1660-1903, B 1660-1936 (CRO, Manchester Local Hist Lib, Runcorn Lib)

RUNCORN Holy Trinity created a parish in 1840 from All Saints
OR C 1838-1945, M 1861-1959 (CRO)
BT 1838-48, 1851, 1854-68 (CRO)

RUNCORN St Michael and All Angels created a parish in 1931 from All Saints
OR C 1922-46, B 1894-1941 (CRO); M 1885+ (Inc)

RUNCORN Preston Brook (Primitive Methodist: Runcorn Circuit) f 1810
OR ZC 1823-37 (PRO: RG 4/543); C 1843-1924 (Circuit) (CRO)
Cop (Mf) ZC 1823-37 (CRO, SLC)

RUNCORN St John's Chapel (Countess of Huntingdon's Connexion) f 1818, sold 1849 to Welsh Presbyterians
OR ZC 1819-37 (PRO: RG 4/195)
Cop (Mf) ZC 1819-37 (CRO, SLC)

RUNCORN Preston Brook (Wesleyan Methodist: Warrington Circuit) f 1819, closed 1970
OR ZC 1818-35 (PRO: RG 4/2397); C 1853-1968 (CRO)
Cop (Mf) ZC 1818-35 (CRO, SLC)

RUNCORN Brunswick Chapel (Wesleyan Methodist: Warrington Circuit) f 1827, replaced by **St Paul**, High Street, 1865 (q.v.), sold 1952
OR ZC 1821-37 (PRO: RG 4/2152)
Cop (Mf) ZC 1821-37 (CRO, SLC)

RUNCORN St Luke, Mason Street (Independent) b 1830 (K 1928)

RUNCORN Bethesda Chapel now Hallwood Chapel, High Street (Independent) b 1835
OR C 1832-39, 1911-45, M 1911, B 1936 (CRO)

RUNCORN Regent Street later (1871) Greenway Road (Primitive Methodist) b 1838, reb 1871, closed 1970
OR C 1924-70 (CRO)

RUNCORN Halton Road (Wesleyan Methodist) f 1842 as **Zion Chapel**, b 1871
OR C 1876-1956, M 1890-1923 (CRO)

RUNCORN St Edward, Irwell Lane or Ivy Street (Roman Catholic) f 1842 b 1888 (K 1928)

RUNCORN Rutland Street (Welsh Calvinist) f 1850 (K 1928)

RUNCORN Ellesmere Street (Wesleyan Methodist) closed 1958
OR C 1850-1954 (CRO)

RUNCORN Camden Chapel, Lowland Road (Wesleyan Methodist) b 1862, closed 1970
OR C 1877-1970, M 1938-70 (CRO)

RUNCORN St Paul, High Street (Wesleyan Methodist) b 1865 replacing **Brunswick Chapel**, closed 1963
OR C 1919-62, M 1848-1961 (CRO)

RUNCORN Clifton Chapel (Primitive Methodist) b 1882, closed 1975
OR C 1936-69 (CRO)

RUNCORN Ashridge Street Chapel (Primitive Methodist) b 1897, closed 1908

RUNCORN Meeting House (Society of Friends) b 1920. From 1802 to 1837 Runcorn was in Lancashire Quarterly Meeting.
OR see Cheshire Quaker Registers; Lancashire Quaker Registers

RUNCORN Victoria Road (Presbyterian) (K 1928)

RUNCORN High Street (Salvation Army) (K 1928)

RUNCORN Laburnum Grove Chapel (Methodist) b 1966, closed 1970
OR C 1960-69 (CRO)

RUNCORN Heath Chapel (Methodist) b 1970

RUNCORN Hallwood Ecumenical Church, Lapwing Grove (United Reformed Church) f 1976, *fl.* 1991

RUNCORN GRANGE St Andrew created a parish in 1963 from Halton
OR CM 1963+ (Inc)

RUNCORN WESTON St John the Evangelist created a parish in 1842 from Runcorn All Saints
OR CM 1842+ (Inc)

RUSHTON township in Tarporley (330)

SAIGHTON township in Chester St Oswald (303)

SALE St Anne (1,104) township in Ashton under Mersey, created a parish in 1856
OR C 1856-1965, M 1857-1974, Banns 1964-87 (CRO)
BT 1856-76 (+ index C 1873-76) (CRO)
Cop (Mf) C 1856-1914, M 1857-1906 (CRO)

SALE St Paul created a parish in 1884 from St Anne
OR CM 1884+ (Inc)

SALE Montague Road (Independent) f 1805
OR with Ch Sec

SALE St Joseph, Hope Road (Roman Catholic) f 1866

SALE Raglan Road (Baptist) f 1875, *fl.* 1989

SALTERFORD or SALTERSFORD St John the Baptist alias Jenkin's Chapel created a parish in 1780 from Prestbury, united to Kettleshulme, 1864
OR C 1770-1821, M 1865-1921, B 1783-1821 (CRO) (for other registers *see* Rainow)
BT 1813-34, 1855, 1860, 1890 (CRO)

SANDBACH St Mary (7,214) [part Northwich Hundred, part Nantwich Hundred; Congleton Union]
OR C 1562-1893, M 1562-1911, Banns 1754-1812, B 1562-1894 (CRO)
BT 1576, 1586, 1593, 1597, 1600, 1604, 1607-12, 1614-15, 1617-21, 1623, 1625-30, 1633-37, 1639-40, 1660-66, 1668-76, 1679-82, 1684-85, 1689-1834, 1836-64 (CRO)
Cop 1562-1808 (Chester AS); 1602-1769 (Chester City Lib); M 1813-37 (NCMI); M 1670-75, 1787-1833, 1835-37 (CMI)
Cop (Mf) C 1562-1893, M 1562-1911, B 1562-1894 (CRO, Manchester Local Hist Lib); C 1799-1837, M 1736-43, 1754-1812 (SG)

SANDBACH Middlewich Road later (1871) Wesley Avenue (Wesleyan Methodist: Congleton Circuit) f 1788
OR ZC 1834-38 (PRO: RG 4/417)
Cop (Mf) ZC 1834-38 (CRO, SLC)

SANDBACH Hope Street (Independent, later United Reformed Church) f 1807, *fl.* 1991
OR ZC 1799-1837 (PRO: RG 4/217)
Cop (Mf) ZC 1799-1837 (CRO, Manchester Local Hist Lib, SLC)

SANDBACH Hassall Green, Betchton (Wesleyan Methodist) f 1829, b 1858
OR C 1838-1952 (CRO)

SANDBACH Union Street later (1857) Welles Street (Primitive Methodist) b 1832, closed 1950
OR M 1911-46 (CRO)

SANDBACH Holmes Chapel, Knutsford Road, Cranage (Wesleyan Methodist: Northwich Circuit) b 1813, f 1830, closed 1900 and replaced
OR ZC 1834-37 (PRO: RG 4/164); C 1844-1973 (chapel), C 1838-1956 (Circuit)
Cop (Mf) ZC 1834-37 (CRO, SLC)

SANDBACH Bradwell Road (Wesleyan Methodist: Wilsford and Sandbach Circuit) (Lewis 1831) b 1882 (K 1928)

SANDBACH Providence Chapel, Bradwall Road (United Methodist) b 1839, closed 1964
OR C 1863-1964, M 1910-63 (CRO)

SANDBACH Sandbach Heath (Wesleyan Methodist) b 1851, closed 1902

SANDBACH Betchton, Malkins Bank (Primitive Methodist) b 1859, closed 1969
OR C 1843-1946 (Circuit) (CRO)

SANDBACH St Winefride, Middlewich Road (Roman Catholic) f 1865 b 1913 (K 1928)

SANDBACH Seaman's Bank (Wesleyan Methodist) (K 1928)

SANDBACH HEATH St John the Evangelist created a parish in 1861 from Sandbach
OR CMB 1861+ (Inc)
BT 1861-64 (CRO)

SANDIWAY St John the Evangelist created a parish in 1935 from Whitegate, Delamere and Weaverham
OR C 1921-35, M 1906-56, Banns 1906-35 (CRO)

SANKEY BRIDGE St James chapelry in Lancashire, transferred to Cheshire, 1974

SANKEY, GREAT St Mary the Virgin parochial chapelry in Lancashire, transferred to Cheshire, 1974 *see* Lancashire NIPR

SAUGHALL, GREAT Grove Chapel Burial Ground
OR B 1868-1983 (Chester RO)

SAUGHALL, GREAT All Saints (367) township in Shotwick, created a parish in 1921
OR CM 1891+ (Inc)

SAUGHALL, LITTLE township in Shotwick (40)

SAUGHALL MASSIE township in Bidston (143)

SEACOMBE St Paul created a parish in 1847 from Wallasey
OR C 1847-1953, M 1848-1954, Banns 1930-58 (CRO)
BT 1851, 1885 (+ index C 1885) (CRO)

SEACOMBE Liscard Road (Independent) (Lewis 1831) b 1905

SEACOMBE Liscard Road (Welsh Presbyterian) f 1837 (K 1924)

SEACOMBE Brighton Street (Wesleyan Methodist: Wallasey Circuit) b 1859 (K 1946)

SEACOMBE Our Lady and St Joseph, Wheatland Lane, Seacombe (Roman Catholic) f 1860

SEACOMBE St Paul's Road Chapel b 1884 (United Methodist: St Domingo Circuit) (K 1924)

SEACOMBE Liscard Road and Brougham Road (Presbyterian, later United Reformed Church) f 1862 b 1912, *fl.* 1991

SEACOMBE Poulton Road (Primitive Methodist: First Circuit) (K 1924) destroyed in World War II

SEVEN OAKS township in Great Budworth (149)

SHAVINGTON cum GRESTY township in Wybunbury (320)

SHIPBROOK township in Davenham (83)

SHOCKLACH St Edith (431) [Broxton Hundred; Wrexham Union 1837-94, Tarvin Union 1894-1930]
OR C 1538-1979, M 1538-1979, Banns 1825-1933, B 1538-1981 (CRO)
BT 1585, 1588, 1599, 1601, 1603-06, 1610-11, 1613-15, 1617-18, 1622-31, 1633-34, 1639, 1664, 1666-69, 1671-72, 1676-77, 1679-85, 1694, 1697-1706, 1708-60, 1763-1800, 1804-22, 1825-40, 1864-90 (+ index CB 1873-89, B 1890) (CRO)
Cop M 1680-85, 1763-1800, 1804-37 (CMI)
Cop (Mf) C 1538-1979, M 1538-1979, B 1538-1981 (CRO, Manchester Local Hist Lib)

SHOCKLACH Shocklach Oviatt (United Methodist) b 1890 (K 1928)

SHOCKLACH OVIATT township in Shocklach

SHOTWICK St Michael and All Angels (713) [Wirral Hundred; Great Boughton Union 1837-53, Hawarden Union 1853-71, Chester Union 1871-1930]
OR C 1681-1991, M 1681-1992, Banns 1754-1812, 1836-1965, B 1681-1992 (CRO)
BT 1591, 1599-1600, 1605, 1607-11, 1614-15, 1617-18, 1622-24, 1626-27, 1630-32, 1634, 1636-39, 1641-42, 1658-60, 1668-72, 1675-76, 1679-82, 1685, 1690-91, 1694-1737, 1739, 1741, 1735-68, 1770-1805, 1807-96 (+ index CB 1873-89) (CRO)
Cop 1681-1775 (Ms CRO); 1690-1723 (Chester City Lib)

SHOTWICK Great Saughall (Presbyterian) (K 1928)

SHOTWICK Church of Christ or Grove Chapel, Great Saughall (Baptist) b 1849, closed 1981
OR C 1845-1947 (CRO)

SHOTWICK Ebenezer Chapel (Primitive Methodist) (K 1928)

SHOTWICK PARK extra-parochial adjacent to Shotwick (18)

SHURLACH township in Davenham (98)

SIDDINGTON All Saints (479) township in Prestbury, created a parish in 1728 [Macclesfield Hundred; Macclesfield Union]
OR CB 1722+, M 1722-54, 1783, 1883+ (Inc)
BT 1722-41, 1745-1863 (CRO)
Cop M 1722-83 (Ptd, Phil 5, 1913); C 1722-1970, M 1722-83 (Ms CRO); M 1722-83 (Boyd); M 1722-54 (CMI, NCMI)

SIDDINGTON (Wesleyan Methodist) b 1865, *fl.* 1979

SMALLWOOD St John the Baptist (554) township in Astbury, created a parish in 1848 [Northwich Hundred; Congleton Union]
OR CMB 1857+ (Inc)
BT 1857-76 (+ index CB 1873-76) (CRO)

SMALLWOOD (Wesleyan Methodist) f 1811
OR C 1920-76 (CRO)

SNELSON township in Rostherne (136)

SOMERFORD All Saints township in Astbury
OR B 1691-1982 (CRO)
Cop (Mf) B 1691-1982 (CRO, Manchester Local Hist Lib)

SOMERFORD BOOTHS township in Astbury (297)

SOUND township in Acton (255)

SPITAL BOUGHTON extra-parochial place [Chester Borough; Chester Union]

SPROSTON township in Middlewich (128)

SPURSTOW township in Bunbury (588)

STALYBRIDGE Before 1889, parts of Stalybridge were in Mottram in Longendale and Stockport, parts in Ashton under Lyne, Lancashire

STALYBRIDGE Old St George, Cocker Hill (12,000) created a parish in 1798 from Ashton under Lyne, Lancashire
OR C 1865-1906. M 1864-1906 (Manchester Local Hist Lib); C 1776+, B 1777+ (Inc)
BT 1782-1820 (Lancs RO)
Cop (Mf) CB 1776-1865 (Manchester Local Hist Lib, Tameside Lib)

STALYBRIDGE Holy Trinity
OR C 1852-1925, M 1852-1933, Banns 1916-48, B 1853-79 (CRO)
BT 1892-93 (CRO)

STALYBRIDGE New St George created a parish in 1847 from Ashton under Lyne, Lancs
OR M 1841-1901 (Manchester Local Hist Lib); CB 1840+ (Inc)

STALYBRIDGE St Paul township 'Stayley' in Mottram, created a parish in 1840
OR C 1839-1960, M 1841-1965, B 1839-1967 (CRO)
BT 1782-90, 1793-95, 1798-1820 (Lancs RO)
Cop (Mf) C 1839-94, M 1841-1908, B 1839-89 (CRO)

STALYBRIDGE Christ Church *see* **DUKINFIELD Christ Church**

STALYBRIDGE Bethel Chapel (Methodist New Connexion) b 1831
OR C 1798-1837 (PRO: RG 4/196, 418); C 1838-1956, M 1838-55, 1899-1956 (Manchester Local Hist Lib)
Cop (Mf) C 1798-1837 (CRO, Manchester Local Hist Lib, SLC)

STALYBRIDGE Ebenezer Chapel (Particular Baptist) f 1813, b 1836 (K 1928)
OR Z 1807-37 (PRO: RG 4/2439)
Cop (Mf) Z 1807-37 (Lancs RO, SLC)

STALYBRIDGE Mount Pleasant or Mount Olivet Chapel, Cross Street later Wakefield Road (General Baptist) f 1804, b 1819, reb 1846 (K 1928)
OR Z 1809-37 (PRO: RG 4/1164); B 1846-1939 (Tameside Lib)
Cop (Mf) Z 1809-37 (Lancs RO, SLC)

STALYBRIDGE Caroline Street (Wesleyan Methodist: Ashton under Lyme Circuit) f 1762, b 1815, reb 1872 (K 1928)
OR C 1812-37, B 1823-37 (PRO: RG 4/545-547)
Cop (Mf) C 1812-37, B 1823-37 (Lancs RO, SLC)

STALYBRIDGE Grasscroft Street and Canal Street (Primitive Methodist) f 1827 b 1892 (K 1928)

STALYBRIDGE Melbourne Street (Independent) b 1830, reb 1861 (K 1928)
OR C 1831-37, B 1834-1837 (PRO: RG 4/2398, 2521); some records 1831-1974 (Tameside Lib)
Cop (Mf) C 1834-37, B 1789-1837 (CRO, Manchester Local Hist Lib, SLC)

STALYBRIDGE St Peter, Spring Bank Street (Roman Catholic) b 1838 (K 1928)

STALYBRIDGE Grosvenor Square (United Methodist) (K 1928)
OR C 1839-42 (Tameside Lib)

STALYBRIDGE Booth Street (United Methodist) b 1849, reb 1877 (K 1928)

STALYBRIDGE Canal Street (Unitarian) f 1860, b 1870 (K 1928)

STALYBRIDGE Portland Street later called Blandford Street (Wesleyan Methodist) b 1864, sold to Presbyterians, 1869

STALYBRIDGE Millbrook (Wesleyan Methodist) (K 1928)

STALYBRIDGE Mount Tabor Chapel, Millbrook (United Methodist) (K 1928)

STALYBRIDGE Castle Street Spiritualist Church, Castle Street (K 1928)

STALYBRIDGE St Raphael, Millbrook (Roman Catholic) f 1958

STANLOW extra-parochial place [Wirral Hundred; Great Boughton Union 1837-71, Chester Union 1871-1930] (13)

STANNEY, GREAT extra-parochial place, incorporated in Ellesmere Port, 1964 [Eddisbury Hundred; Great Boughton Union 1837-71, Chester Union 1871-1930] (32)

STANNEY, LITTLE township in Stoke (201)

STANTHORNE township in Davenham (149)

STAPELEY township in Wybunbury (356)

STAPLEFORD, BRUEN township in Tarvin (159)

STAPLEFORD, FOULK township in Tarvin (244)

STAYLEY township in Mottram (2,440), later **STALYBRIDGE** (q.v.)

STOAK *see* **STOKE**

STOCKHAM township in Runcorn (52)

STOCKPORT Board of Guardians
OR Vaccinations 1871-99, 1901-02, D 1874-95 (Stockport Lib)

STOCKPORT Cemetery, Heaviley, opened 1838 (50 acres)

STOCKPORT Willow Grove Cemetery, Reddish, opened 1877 (17 acres)

STOCKPORT St Mary the Virgin [Macclesfield Hundred; Stockport Union]
OR C 1584-1890, M 1584-1892, Banns 1788-93, 1807-12, 1816-19, 1830-52, 1887-1955, B 1584-1909 (CRO)
BT 1605, 1610-11, 1617-24, 1626-41, 1663-85, 1687-90, 1695-97, 1699-1715, 1718, 1721-28, 1730-48, 1750-69, 1771-1833, 1837, 1839-44 (CRO)
Cop 1584-1620 (Ptd, E.W. Bulkeley, 1889); M 1834-36 (Ptd, *Manchester Genealogist* 5:2, 1969); 1584-1626 (Ptd, Cheshire N & Q 6-9, 1886-89); 1619-27 (Ptd, *Cheshire N & Q* New Series 2, 1897); 1620-80 (John Rylands Lib, Manchester); 1627-40 (Stockport Lib); M 1822-81 (Manchester Local Hist Lib); M 1799-1837 (SG); B 1746-62 (Ts CRO); M 1584-1837 (NCMI); M 1730-66 (CMI)
Cop (Mf) C 1584-1890, M 1584-1892, B 1584-1909 (CRO, Manchester Local Hist Lib, Stockport Lib); C 1782-1805, 1818-26, 1847-49, M 1737-1815, 1847-49 (SG); M 1799-1837 (Ptd, Manchester and Lancashire Family History Society, 1988)

STOCKPORT St Peter, St Peter's Square f 1768 created a parish in 1840 from St Mary
OR C 1816+, MB 1840+ (Inc)
Cop C 1816-1935 (Stockport Lib)

STOCKPORT St Thomas, Wellington Road South, created a parish in 1827 from St Mary
OR C 1837-93, M 1875-95, Banns 1924-63, B 1825-56 (CRO)
Cop M 1875-1926 (Stockport Lib)
Cop (Mf) C 1837-93, M 1875-95, B 1825-56 (CRO, Manchester Local Hist Lib)

STOCKPORT St Paul *see* **PORTWOOD St Paul**

STOCKPORT St Saviour, Store Street created a parish in 1934 from St George and St Alban
OR CM 1855+ (Inc)

STOCKPORT St Matthew, Grenville Street, created a parish in 1844 from St Thomas
OR C 1858-1911, M 1858-1900 (CRO)

STOCKPORT St Augustine, Stockport Road created from St Matthew and Cheadle Heath b 1893
OR C 1887-1950, M 1894-1947 (CRO)

STOCKPORT St Alban, Hall Street created a parish in 1893 from St Mary and Bredbury
OR C 1877-1963, M 1900-51, Banns 1899-1928, 1939-62 (CRO)

STOCKPORT St George, St Peter and St Mark created a parish in 1897 from St Thomas
OR C 1897-1984, M 1897-1985, Banns 1897-1989 (CRO)

STOCKPORT St Mark, Berlin Road, Edgeley, created a parish in 1911 from St Matthew
OR CM 1911+ (Inc)

STOCKPORT Meeting House, Lower Hillgate (Society of Friends) f 17th century, b 1705 (K 1928)
OR see Cheshire Quaker Registers

STOCKPORT Old Chapel or Tabernacle, Middle Hillgate (Independent) f 1672 (K 1928)
<u>OR</u> C 1709-93, 1801-36, B 1807-36 (PRO: RG 4/420, 2023); C 1709-1837 (Manchester Local Hist Lib)
<u>Cop</u> (Mf) C 1709-93, 1801-36, B 1807-36 (CRO, Manchester Local Hist Lib, SLC)

STOCKPORT Hatherlow (Independent) f 1706
<u>OR</u> ZC 1785-1837, B 1793-1837 (PRO: RG 4/577, 2091, 2260-61); ZC 1732-81, 1785-1837, B 1793-1837 (Manchester Local Hist Lib)
<u>Cop</u> C 1732-81 (Ptd, G.R. Axon, *Transactions of the Lancashire and Cheshire Archaeological Society* 44, 1927); C 1732-81 (Ptd, *South Cheshire Family History Society Quarterly Journal* 4, 1991)
<u>Cop</u> (Mf) ZC 1785-1837, B 1793-1837 (CRO, SLC)

STOCKPORT Hyde Chapel (Presbyterian)
<u>OR</u> ZC 1710-1838, B 1785-1837 (PRO: RG 4/98-99, 171, 548-49, 2262)
<u>Cop</u> (Mf) ZC 1710-1838, B 1785-1837 (CRO, SLC)

STOCKPORT High Street Chapel, St Peters Gate (Unitarian) f 1723 b 1842 (K 1928)
<u>OR</u> C 1761-1837, B 1780-1835 (PRO: 197-199, 419, 1800-01)
<u>Cop</u> (Mf) C 1761-1837, B 1780-1835 (CRO, SLC)

STOCKPORT Old or Hillgate Chapel, Hillgate later (1807) Park Street (Wesleyan Methodist) f 1759, closed 1825
<u>OR</u> C 1793-1838 (Stockport Lib)

STOCKPORT Church Gate Chapel, Orchard Street, Waterloo Road (Independent) f 1786, b 1788, closed 1907
<u>OR</u> ZC 1788-1837 (PRO: RG 4/421-22, 551); C 1788-1811, 1822-37 (Manchester Local Hist Lib)
<u>Cop</u> (Mf) ZC 1788-1837 (CRO, SLC)

STOCKPORT Bethesda Chapel, Ratcliffe Street (Independent Methodist) b 1832
<u>OR</u> C 1797-1919, B 1833-47 (Stockport Lib)
<u>Cop</u> C 1797-1919 (Ts Index CRO)

STOCKPORT London Square (Wesleyan New Connexion) b 1798, closed 1865 and replaced by **Mount Tabor Chapel** (q.v.)

STOCKPORT Our Lady and the Apostles, Edgeley (Roman Catholic) f 1799 b 1905 (K 1928)

STOCKPORT Hanover Chapel, New Road, Lancashire Hill, Heaton Mersey (Independent) f 1815, b 1842
<u>OR</u> C 1816-1961 (CRO)

STOCKPORT Providence Chapel, Heaton Lane (Baptist) b 1817, *fl.* 1850

STOCKPORT Windmill Room, Edward Street (Independent) f 1817, closed 1820
<u>OR</u> ZC 1818-37 (PRO: RG 4/7)
<u>Cop</u> (Mf) ZC 1818-37 (CRO, Manchester Local Hist Lib, SLC)

STOCKPORT Castle Street, Edgeley (Wesleyan Methodist: Trinity Circuit) b 1818, reb 1873 (K 1928)

STOCKPORT Ebenezer Chapel, St Peter's Place or Duke Street (Primitive Methodist: First Circuit) f 1827, moved to Wellington Road South, 1880 (K 1928)
<u>OR</u> ZC 1831-37 (PRO: RG 4/550)
<u>Cop</u> (Mf) ZC 1831-37 (CRO, SLC)

STOCKPORT Great Portwood Street (United Methodist) b 1835 (K 1928)

STOCKPORT Thomson Street (Baptist) b 1838, *fl.* 1989

STOCKPORT Zion Chapel, Greek Street (Baptist) b 1840 (K 1928)

STOCKPORT Brunswick Chapel, Portwood (Wesleyan Methodist: Tiviot Dale Circuit) b 1849
OR C 1849-1954, M 1850-1900 (Stockport Lib)

STOCKPORT Dean Row (Wesleyan Methodist) b 1849

STOCKPORT Covent Garden (Latter-Day Saints) (met at Wellington Steps, 1850, but not continuous congregation) (K 1928)

STOCKPORT Tiviot Dale (Wesleyan Methodist: Tiviot Dale Circuit) (K 1928)
OR M 1851-99 (Stockport Lib)

STOCKPORT St Joseph, Tatton Street (Roman Catholic) f 1851 b 1862 (K 1928)

STOCKPORT Mount Tabor Chapel, Wellington Road South replacing earlier chapel in London Square (United Methodist) b 1865, reb 1879 (K 1928)

STOCKPORT Wellington Road South (Independent) b 1866 (K 1928)

STOCKPORT Union Chapel, Offerton Lane (Independent) b 1872 (K 1928)

STOCKPORT Bethesda Chapel (Wesleyan Methodist)
OR C 1872-1967 (Stockport Lib)

STOCKPORT Heaton Moor Road (Wesleyan Methodist: Tiviot Dale Circuit) b 1873 (K 1928)

STOCKPORT Davenport Chapel, Bramhall Lane (Baptist) f 1878, *fl.* 1989

STOCKPORT Trinity Chapel, Bramall Lane later Wellington Road South (Wesleyan Methodist: Trinity Circuit) b 1885 (K 1928)

STOCKPORT Woodley (Primitive Methodist: Woodley Circuit) *fl.* 1887 (K 1928)

STOCKPORT Christadelphian Synagogue, Dodgehill Old Road *fl.* 1887 (K 1928)

STOCKPORT Bamford Street (Independent Methodist) *fl.* 1887 (K 1928)

STOCKPORT St Ann, Reddish Road (Wesleyan Methodist: Tiviot Dale Circuit) (K 1928)
OR C 1888-1957 (Stockport Lib)

STOCKPORT Heaton Moor Road (Independent) *fl.* 1892, reb 1896 (K 1928)

STOCKPORT St Mary, Our Lady of the Rosary, Roman Road, Norris Bank b 1897 (K 1928)

STOCKPORT Hollywood Park (Wesleyan Methodist)
OR C 1899-1948 (Stockport Lib)

STOCKPORT Buxton Road (Independent) b 1900 (K 1928)

STOCKPORT Heaton Mersey (Wesleyan Methodist) b 1906 (K 1928)

STOCKPORT Newbridge Lane (Wesleyan Methodist)
OR C 1914-39 (Stockport Lib)

STOCKPORT Broadstone Road, Reddish (Wesleyan Methodist) (K 1928)

STOCKPORT Bethel Chapel, Millgate (Old Baptist Union) (K 1928)

STOCKPORT Synagogue, Chestergate (Jewish) (K 1928)

STOCKPORT St Andrew, Heaton Moor Road (Presbyterian) (K 1928)

STOCKPORT Wycliffe Chapel, Wellington Road North (Independent) (K 1928)

STOCKPORT Edgeley Road (Independent) (K 1928)

STOCKPORT Brinksway (Independent) (K 1928)

STOCKPORT Didsbury Road (Independent) (K 1928)

STOCKPORT Broadstone Road, Reddish (Independent) (K 1928)

STOCKPORT St Joseph, Gorton Road, Reddish (Roman Catholic)

STOCKPORT Wellington Road South (Primitive Methodist: First Circuit) (K 1928)

STOCKPORT Edgeley Road (Primitive Methodist: First Circuit) (K 1928)

STOCKPORT Manchester Road (Primitive Methodist: Second Circuit) (K 1928)

STOCKPORT St John, Stockport Road (United Methodist) (K 1928)

STOCKPORT Cheadle Heath (United Methodist) (K 1928)

STOCKPORT Edgeley Park (United Methodist) (K 1928)

STOCKPORT Wellington Street (Welsh Calvinist Methodist) (K 1928)

STOCKPORT Broadstone Road, Reddish (Wesleyan Methodist: Tiviot Dale Circuit) (K 1928)

STOCKPORT Didsbury Road, Heaton Mersey (Wesleyan Methodist: Tiviot Dale Circuit) (K 1928)

STOCKPORT Middle Hillgate (Salvation Army) (K 1928)

STOCKPORT Mottram Street (Salvation Army) (K 1928)

STOCKPORT Crowther Street (Progressive Society of Spiritualists) (K 1928)

STOCKPORT Central Spiritualist Church, Lord Street (K 1928)

STOCKPORT Spiritualist Church, Higher Hillgate (K 1928)

STOCKPORT St Ambrose, Adswood Road, Adswood (Roman Catholic) f 1939

STOCKPORT St Bernardette, Brinnington (Roman Catholic) f 1957

STOCKTON township in Malpas (30)

STOCKTON HEATH St Thomas created a parish in 1838 from Great Budworth, Runcorn and Warrington, Lancashire
OR C 1838-1947, M 1841-1941, B 1839-1944 (CRO)
BT 1838-44 (CRO)
Cop (Mf) C 1838-1963, M 1841-1903, B 1839-1868 (CRO, Manchester Local Hist Lib)

STOCKTON HEATH (Independent Methodist) f 1807 (K 1928)
OR ZC 1815-55 (PRO: RG 4/3534)
Cop (Mf) ZC 1815-55 (CRO, SLC)

STOCKTON HEATH (Wesleyan Methodist) (K 1928)

STOCKTON HEATH (Primitive Methodist) (K 1928)

STOCKTON HEATH Our Lady, Dingle Way, Appleton (Roman Catholic) (Cath Dir 1965)

STOKE alias STOAK St Laurence (334) [Wirral Hundred; Great Boughton Union 1837-71, Chester Union 1871-1930]
OR C 1573-1925, M 1573-1993, Banns 1754-1812, B 1573-1889 (CRO)
BT 1607, 1610, 1613-15, 1618, 1619?, 1621-24, 1626-27, 1630, 1632-34, 1636-38, 1640-41, 1666, 1668-76, 1679-85, 1690-91, 1712-16, 1718-27, 1730-37, 1739, 1741-1841, 1843-45 (CRO)
Cop M 1711-39, 1755-1837 (CMI)
Cop (Mf) C 1573-1925, M 1573-1964, B 1573-1889 (CRO, Manchester Local Hist Lib)

STOKE township in Acton (124)

STORETON township in Bebington (192)

STRETTON St Matthew (324) chapelry in Great Budworth, created a parish in 1830 [Bucklow Hundred; Runcorn Union]
OR C 1827-1944, M 1835-1938, B 1828-1960 (CRO)
BT 1827-51, 1896-99 (CRO)
Cop M 1835-37 (CMI)
Cop (Mf) C 1827-1914, M 1835-1938, B 1828-1921 (CRO)

STRETTON township in Tilston (105)

STUBLACH township in Middlewich (66)

STYAL town in Pownall Fee, Wilmslow

SUTTON St George (5,836) created a parish in 1835 from Prestbury
OR C 1823-81, M 1835-83, Banns 1835-61 (CRO)
Cop M 1835-37 (NCMI)
Cop (Mf) C 1823-81, M 1835-83 (CRO, Manchester Local Hist Lib)

SUTTON township in Middlewich (18)

SUTTON township in Runcorn (237)

SUTTON, GREAT St John the Evangelist (162) township in Eastham, created a parish in 1880
OR C 1879-1940, Banns 1880-1947 (CRO); MB 1879+ (Inc)

SUTTON, GUILDEN *see* **GUILDEN SUTTON**

SUTTON LANE ENDS St James (created from Prestbury, 1859)
<u>OR</u> CMB 1840+ (Inc)

SUTTON LANE ENDS Langley (Wesleyan Methodist) b 1858 (K 1928)

SUTTON LANE ENDS Hollin Lane (Wesleyan Methodist) b 1880 (K 1928)

SUTTON LANE ENDS Lane Ends (United Methodist) closed by 1928 (K 1928)

SUTTON, LITTLE township in Eastham (367)

SUTTON, LITTLE Chapel (Wesleyan Methodist: Bebington South Circuit) f 1840, b 1877 (K 1946)

SUTTON, LITTLE St George, New Chester Road (United Reformed Church) f 1835, *fl.*1991

SWETTENHAM St Peter (421) [Northwich Hundred; Congleton Union]
<u>OR</u> C 1547-1890, M 1547-1835, Banns 1754-1812, B 1547-1881 (CRO)
<u>BT</u> 1596, 1604, 1609, 1611, 1615, 1617-18, 1621, 1624, 1626, 1628-30, 1632-34, 1636, 1640-41, 1663-65, 1669-76, 1679-85, 1687-92, 1694-98, 1700-04, 1707-16, 1718, 1720-21, 1724, 1726-30, 1732, 1735-1859 (CRO)
<u>Cop</u> CB 1570-1812, M 1570-1835 (SG); M 1570-1837 (NCMI); M 1701-16, 1740-1837 (CMI)
<u>Cop</u> (Mf) C 1547-1890, M 1547-1835, B 1547-1881 (CRO, Manchester Local Hist Lib)

SWETTENHAM Davenport (Wesleyan Methodist) b 1834 (K 1928)

SWETTENHAM St Thomas and St Mary (Roman Catholic) (K 1928)

TABLEY INFERIOR township in Great Budworth (134)

TABLEY Cemetery, Tabley Hill (6 acres)

TABLEY, OVER St Paul (442) township in Rostherne, created a parish in 1855
<u>OR</u> C 1855-1904, M 1856-1988, Banns 1857-1980 (CRO)
<u>BT</u> 1855-98, 1930-32 (+ index CB 1873-91) (CRO)

TARPORLEY St Helen (2,391) [Eddisbury Hundred and Tarporley Borough; Nantwich Union, 1837-94, Tarvin Union 1894-1930]
<u>OR</u> C 1557-1921, M 1558-1923, Banns 1830-1934, B 1558-1888 (CRO)
<u>BT</u> 1600, 1606, 1608, 1610-12, 1614, 1616-17, 1622-25, 1627-37, 1639-41, 1663, 1668-77, 1679-85, 1688-92, 1694-98, 1700-22, 1724-25, 1727-1864 (CRO)
<u>Cop</u> 1557-1665 (Ms I CRO); 1559-1755 (British Lib, SG); M 1568-82, 1700-24, 1742-53, 1789-1837 (CMI)
<u>Cop</u> (Mf) C 1558-1921, M 1558-1923, B 1558-1888 (CRO, Manchester Local Hist Lib)

TARPORLEY (Wesleyan Methodist) b 1791, reb 1867, closed 1976
<u>OR</u> C 1839-94 (Chester RO); C 1867-88 (Circuit), M 1902-75 (CRO)

TARPORLEY (Baptist) f 1817 b 1866 (K 1928)
<u>OR</u> Z 1801-36 (PRO: RG 4/424)

TARPORLEY Eaton (Wesleyan Methodist) b 1840, *fl.*1958

TARPORLEY Cotebrook (Primitive Methodist) b 1843 (K 1928)

TARPORLEY (Primitive Methodist) b 1846, closed by 1928

TARPORLEY Utkinton (Primitive Methodist) b 1863, *fl.*1959
OR C 1875-1964 (Circuit) (CRO)

TARPORLEY St Thomas à Becket, Nantwich Road and Eaton Road (Roman Catholic) f 1938

TARVIN St Andrew (3,415) [part Eddisbury Hundred, part Broxton Hundred; Great Boughton Union 1837-71, Tarvin Union 1871-1930]
OR C 1563-1926, M 1563-1978, Banns 1832-1984, B 1563-1993 (CRO)
BT 1584, 1601, 1603-06, 1608-12, 1614, 1616, 1619, 1622-25, 1629-34, 1637-38, 1640-41, 1663, 1666-68, 1670-77, 1679-85, 1690-91, 1695, 1697-1877, 1879-1907 (+ index CB 1873-90) (CRO)
Cop M 1563-1688 (Ms CRO); M 1681-88, 1793-1837 (CMI)
Cop (Mf) C 1563-1926, M 1563-1950, B 1563-1951 (CRO, Manchester Local Hist Lib)

TARVIN Mouldsworth (Wesleyan Methodist) b 1816, reb 1887

TARVIN Duddon (Wesleyan Methodist) b 1834, reb 1890, *fl.*1969

TARVIN Trinity Chapel (Wesleyan Methodist) b 1849, reb 1983
OR M 1894-1924 (CRO)

TARVIN Zion Chapel (Primitive Methodist) b 1875, closed 1983
OR C 1876-1928, M 1948-83 (CRO)

TARVIN Clotton Hoofield (Primitive Methodist) b 1886 (K 1928)

TARVIN Pryors Hayes (United Methodist) (K 1928)

TATTENHALL St Alban (1,080) [Broxton Hundred; Great Boughton Union 1837-71; Tarvin Union 1871-1930]
OR C 1654-1942, M 1654-1947, Banns 1823-1962, B 1654-1945 (CRO)
BT 1579, 1585-86, 1593, 1599, 1601, 1604, 1606, 1610, 1613-14, 1618, 1622, 1624, 1639-41, 1664, 1666, 1668-77, 1679-85, 1687-92, 1695-1700, 1710, 1713-32, 1734-41, 1745-60, 1762-1854, 1856-1892 (+ index CB 1873-92) (CRO)
Cop C 1812-35 (Ptd, Index, *Family History Society of Cheshire Journal* 3 (3), 7 (1-2), 1972, 1977-78); CB 1812-35 (SG); M 1690-1700, 1747-1837 (CMI)
Cop (Mf) C 1654-1835, M 1654-1837, B 1654-1856 (CRO, Manchester Local Hist Lib)

TATTENHALL (Independent) b 1796 (K 1928)
OR C 1798-1853, 1955-62, M 1955-62, B 1955-62 (CRO)

TATTENHALL Tattenhall Lanes (Wesleyan Methodist) b before 1800, closed 1937

TATTENHALL Tattenhall Lanes (Primitive Methodist) b 1809, reb 1898, closed 1979
OR M 1926-79 (CRO)

TATTON township in Rostherne (69)

TAXAL St Leonard later TAXALL St James (662) parish in Cheshire but part transferred to Derbyshire as Whaley Bridge civil parish, 1936 [Macclesfield Hundred; Macclesfield Union]
OR C 1610-1867, M 1610-1894, B 1610-1894 (CRO)
BT 1599,1605,1663-65,1668-74,1676,1678-85,1693-94,1712,1715,1717-23,1726-27, 1729-1813,1815,1818-78 (+ index CB 1873-78) (CRO)
Cop CB 1610-1837 (Ts I CRO); M 1611-1812 (Ptd, Phil 1, 1909); M 1813-37 (Ptd, Phil 5, 1913); C 1611-1804, M 1613-1826, B 1611-1838 (Chester AS); CB 1873-78 (Ms I CRO); M 1651-75, 1701-50, 1776-1837 (Boyd); M 1611-1837 (NCMI); M 1813-37 (CMI)

TAXAL Kettleshulme (Wesleyan Methodist: Buxton Circuit) (originally in Prestbury, but transferred to Taxal in 1922) b 1815, reb 1901 (K 1936)
OR ZC 1808-36 (PRO: RG 4/2092)
Cop (Mf) ZC 1808-36 (CRO, SLC)

TAXAL Yeardsley (Wesleyan Methodist) (Lewis 1831)

TAXAL Whaley Bridge (Wesleyan Methodist) f 1820 (K 1936)
OR ZC 1827-37 (PRO: RG 4/3532)
Cop (Mf) ZC 1827-37 (CRO, SLC)

TAXAL Whaley Bridge (Independent) b 1869 (K 1936)

TAXAL Whaley Bridge (Independent) b 1869 (K 1936)

TAXAL The Sacred Heart, Whaley Lane, Whaley Bridge (Roman Catholic) f 1900 b 1902 (K 1936)

TAXAL Whaley Bridge (Baptist) (K 1936)

TAXAL Furness Vale, Whaley Bridge (United Methodist) (K 1928)

TETTON township in Warmingham (181)

THELWALL All Saints (332) chapelry in Runcorn, created a parish in 1737 [Bucklow Hundred; Runcorn Union 1836-45, Warrington Union 1845-1930]
OR C 1782-1863, M 1846-1981, B 1784-1915 (CRO)
BT 1812-33, 1835-36, 1839-45, 1847, 1855 (CRO)

THINGWALL township in Woodchurch (77)

THORNTON, CHILDER township in Eastham (296)

THORNTON HOUGH All Saints (144) township in Neston, created a parish in 1869 from Willaston and Neston
OR C 1868-1902 (CRO); MB 1868+ (Inc)
BT 1868-77 (+ index CB 1873-77) (CRO)

THORNTON HOUGH St George (Independent, later United Reformed Church) b 1903, *fl.*1991

THORNTON le MOORS St Mary (914) [Eddisbury Hundred; Great Boughton Union 1837-71, Chester Union 1871-1930]
OR C 1574-1901, M 1574-1837, Banns 1754-1812, 1824-1903, B 1574-1898 (CRO)
BT 1588, 1601, 1611, 1614-17, 1623, 1625, 1627-35, 1637, 1639-41, 1663, 1666, 1668-77, 1679-82, 1684, 1689-91, 1694-1701, 1703-61, 1763-1891 (+ index CB 1873-91) (CRO)
Cop 1641-42, 1663-64, 1676, 1769-70, 1774-77, 1782 (BT) (CRO); M 1574-1753 (Ts CRO); M 1707-13, 1729-37, 1755-1837 (CMI)
Cop (Mf) C 1574-1901, M 1574-1837, B 1574-1898 (CRO, Manchester Local Hist Lib)

THORNTON le MOORS Elton (Primitive Methodist) (K 1928)

THORNTON le MOORS Dunham on the Hill (Wesleyan Methodist) (K 1928)

THORNTON le MOORS Dunham on the Hill (Wesleyan Methodist) (K 1928)

THREAPWOOD St John extra-parochial place, created a parish in 1968 [part Maylor Hundred, Flintshire, part Broxton Hundred, Cheshire, made all Cheshire in 1896; Wrexham Union 1838-94, Whitchurch Union 1894-1930]
OR C 1817-1944, M 1837-1966, Banns 1889-1978, B 1829-1989 (CRO)
BT 1817-40 (CRO)
Cop M 1832-33 (CMI)

THREAPWOOD (Independent) b 1850 (K 1928) closed by 1988

THURSTASTON St Bartholomew (92) [Wirral Hundred; Wirral Union]
OR C 1706-1907, M 1706-1837, Banns 1754-1812, B 1706-1812 (CRO); B 1813+ (Inc)
BT 1581, 1600, 1603, 1616-19, 1634, 1636, 1638-39, 1663, 1666, 1668-69, 1671, 1673-76, 1679?, 1680-81, 1684, 1695-96, 1698, 1705-39, 1741-1895 (CRO)
Cop 1706-47 (Ts I CRO, SG); M 1756-1837 (CMI)
Cop (Mf) C 1706-1907, M 1706-1837, B 1706-1812 (CRO, Wirral Archives, Manchester Local Hist Lib)

TILSTON St Mary (873) [Broxton Hundred; Great Boughton Union 1837-71, Tarvin Union 1871-1930]
OR C 1558-1937, M 1558-1837, Banns 1754-1812, 1823-1962, B 1558-1924 (CRO)
BT 1585, 1604-05, 1610, 1613, 1615, 1618, 1621-31, 1635, 1664, 1666-77, 1679-85, 1687-91, 1693-97, 1700-42, 1744-1839, 1841 (CRO)
Cop M 1724-1837 (CMI)
Cop (Mf) C 1558-1937, M 1558-1837, B 1558-1924 (CRO, Manchester Local Hist Lib)

TILSTON (Wesleyan Methodist) (K 1928)

TILSTON (Primitive Methodist) (K 1928)

TILSTON FEARNALL St Jude (170) chapelry in Bunbury, created a parish in 1837 [Eddisbury Hundred; Nantwich Union 1837-71, Tarvin Union 1871-1930]
OR C 1838-73, 1889-1901, M 1901-77, B 1848-73, 1889-1901 (CRO)
Cop (Mf) C 1838-73, 1889-1901, B 1848-73, 1889-1901 (CRO)

TIMPERLEY Christ Church (752) township in Bowdon, created a parish in 1852 [Bucklow Hundred; Altrincham Union 1836-95, Bucklow Union 1895-1930]
OR CMB 1849+ (Inc)
BT 1852-88 (+ index CB 1873-88) (CRO)

TINTWISTLE Christ Church (1,820) township in Mottram, created a parish in 1840 [Macclesfield Hundred; Ashton under Lyne Union]
OR C 1837-82, M 1839-84, Banns 1899-1968, B 1837-93 (CRO)
BT 1837-41, 1855 (CRO)

TINTWISTLE Ebenezer Chapel, Old Road (Wesleyan Methodist) b 1830 (K 1928)
OR C 1839-1956 (Manchester Local Hist Lib)

TINTWISTLE (Independent, later United Reformed Church) f 1688 (K 1928)
OR C 1747-1837 (PRO: RG 4/2153, 3533); C 1747-1837, B 1798-1821 (Manchester Local Hist Lib) (entries 1715-47 are in the registers of Mottram in Longdendale)
Cop B 1840-65 (CRO)
Cop (Mf) C 1747-1837 (CRO, SLC)

TITTENLEY township in Audlem (30)

TIVERTON township in Bunbury (618)

TOFT St John the Evangelist (200) township in Knutsford, created a parish in 1854
OR C 1855-1983, M 1856-1983, B 1865-1982 (CRO)
BT C 1855-60 (CRO)

TORKINGTON township in Stockport (284)

TRAFFORD, BRIDGE township in Plemstall (58)

TRAFFORD, MICKLE township in Plemstall (333)

TRAFFORD, WIMBOLDS township in Thornton le Moors (118)

TRANMERE St Catherine, Higher Tranmere (1,168) chapelry in Bebington, created a parish in 1842 [Wirral Hundred; Wirral Union]
OR C 1831-1947, M 1845-1946, Banns 1978-85 (CRO)
Cop (Mf) C 1831-1910, M 1845-1904 (CRO)

TRANMERE St Paul, Old Chester Road, Rock Ferry, created a parish in 1858 from St Catherine
OR C 1858-1959, M 1858-1958, Banns 1858-83, 1909-27, 1971-90 (CRO)
BT 1858-77 (+ index C 1873-77) (CRO)
Cop (Mf) C 1858-1910, M 1858-1903 (CRO)

TRANMERE Wesley Chapel, Church Road, Higher Tranmere (Wesleyan Methodist: Birkenhead Circuit) f 1844, b 1862, reb 1966
OR C 1855-1953 (CRO)

TRANMERE Freehold Chapel, Old Chester Road (Wesleyan Methodist: Birkenhead Circuit) f 1867, b 1890, closed 1954
OR C 1857-1953, M 1905-44 (CRO)

TRANMERE Mount Tabor Chapel, Holt Road, Higher Tranmere (Wesleyan Methodist: Bebington Circuit) b 1862, closed 1965

TRANMERE Mount Tabor Chapel, Holt Road, Higher Tranmere (Primitive Methodist: Second Circuit) b 1872, closed 1965
OR C 1928-61 (CRO)

TRANMERE St Paul, North Road, Devonshire Park, Upper Tranmere (Presbyterian) b 1900 (K 1924-48)

TRANMERE Old Chester Road (Independent, later United Reformed Church) b 1901, *fl.*1991

TRANMERE Park Grove, Whetstone Lane (Particular Baptist) (K 1924)

TRANMERE Willmer Road (English Presbyterian) (K 1924)

TRANMERE Holt Hill Terrace (Church of Christ) (K 1946)

TRANMERE, LOWER St Luke, Old Chester Road, b 1881, created a parish in 1883 from St Catherine
OR C 1883-1970, M 1884-1970, Banns 1883-1903, 1947-53 (CRO)
BT 1883-1901 (+ index CB 1883-91) (CRO)

TUSHINGHAM St Chad (328) township in Malpas, created a parish in 1824 [Broxton Hundred; Nantwich Union 1837-53, Whitchurch Union 1853-1930]
OR CMB 1861+ (Inc)
BT 1861-72 (CRO)

TUSHINGHAM Bradley (Independent) b 1891 (K 1928)

TUSHINGHAM (Primitive Methodist) (K 1928)

TUSHINGHAM Agden (Primitive Methodist) (K 1928)

TWEMLOW township in Sandbach (152)

TYTHERINGTON township in Prestbury (427)

UPTON township in Prestbury (64)

UPTON Landican Cemetery, Arrowe Park Road (K 1946)

UPTON St Mary (by BIRKINHEAD) *see* **OVERCHURCH St Mary**

UPTON near CHESTER Holy Ascension (289) chapelry in Chester St Mary on the Hill from the Dissolution to 1743 [Broxton Hundred; Chester Union]
OR C 1854-1956, M 1875-1986, Banns 1875-1908, 1930-89, B 1853-1976 (CRO)

UPTON Heath Road (Independent, later United Reformed Church) b 1860, *fl.* 1991

UPTON Ford Road (Presbyterian) f 1898 (K 1924-46)

UPTON PRIORY Resurrection

UTKINTON township in Tarporley (564)

WALGHERTON township in Wybunbury (213)

WALLASEY St Hilary [Wirral Hundred; Wirral Union 1836-91, Birkinhead Union 1891-1930]
OR C 1574-1901, M 1574-1903, Banns 1823-69, B 1574-1946 (CRO)
BT 1600, 1603, 1606-10, 1613, 1615, 1617-18, 1622-24, 1626-27, 1630, 1634, 1636, 1658-60, 1666, 1668-71, 1673-74, 1676, 1679-81, 1683-85, 1689-91, 1694-1739, 1741-60, 1762-95, 1797-1878 (+ index CB 1873-78) (CRO)
Cop 1574-1812 (Ts CRO, Liverpool Ref Lib, SG); 1600-1786 (Chester City Lib); M 1695-1717, 1752-1836 (CMI)
Cop (Mf) C 1574-1901, M 1574-1903, B 1574-1946 (CRO, Manchester Local Hist Lib)

WALLASEY Meeting House (Society of Friends) From 1831 to 1837 Wallasey was in Lancashire Quarterly Meeting.
OR see Cheshire Quaker Registers; Lancashire Quaker Registers

WALLASEY St Nicholas (Harrison Memorial Church), Groveland Road, created a parish in 1912 from St Hilary
OR M 1912-26 (CRO); C 1912+ (Inc)

WALLASEY Brighton Street and Victoria Road (Wesleyan Methodist) b 1839, closed 1966
OR M 1902-64 (CRO)

WALLASEY New Brighton Chapel, Rowson Street (Wesleyan Methodist: Wallasey Circuit) b 1870 (K 1946)

WALLASEY St Paul's Road Chapel (United Methodist) b *c*1884, closed 1935
OR C 1909-34 (CRO)

WALLASEY Claremont Road (Wesleyan Methodist: Wallasey Circuit) b 1885, reb 1910 (K 1946)

WALLASEY Manor Road (Wesleyan Methodist) f 1893, b 1904, *fl.* 1962

WALLASEY Oakdale Road (Wesleyan Methodist) f 1899, closed 1943
OR C 1932-35 (CRO)

WALLASEY Wallasey Village (Presbyterian, later United Reformed Church) f 1877 b 1900, *fl.* 1991

WALLASEY English Martyrs, St George's Road (Roman Catholic) f 1902

WALLASEY Poulton Road Chapel (Primitive Methodist) b *c*1904, demolished 1944
OR M 1916-49 (CRO)

WALLASEY Oxton Road Chapel (Wesleyan Methodist) f 1905, reb 1961

WALLASEY Marlowe Road (Independent, later United Reformed Church) b 1913, *fl.* 1991

WALLASEY St Saviour, Radnor Drive (Free Church of England) (K 1924-46)

WALLASEY First Church of Christ, Scientist, St Hilary Brow (Christian Science) (K 1946)

WALLERSCOAT township in Weaverham (10)

WALTON St John the Evangelist created a parish in 1879 from Daresbury and Stockton Heath
OR CM 1879+ (Inc)

WALTON INFERIOR township in Runcorn (346)

WALTON SUPERIOR township in Runcorn (238)

WARBURTON St Werburgh (510) [Bucklow Hundred; Altrincham Union 1837-95, Bucklow Union 1895-1930]
OR C 1611-20, 1632-66, 1674-1935, M 1655-65, 1673-1836 (irregular 1685-1715, 1732-51), B 1638, 1653-1932 (CRO)
BT 1813-14, 1869-76 (+ index CB 1873-76) (CRO)
Cop 1657-1910 (Ms CRO); M 1655-1837 (Boyd); M 1754-1837 (NCMI); M 1715-52, 1801-37 (CMI)
Cop (Mf) C 1611-1859, M 1611-1836, B 1611-1863 (CRO, Manchester Local Hist Lib)

WARDLE township in Bunbury (144)

WARFORD, GREAT township in Alderley (349)

WARMINGHAM St Leonard (1,831) [Northwich Hundred; Nantwich Union]
OR C 1538-1857, M 1538-1907, B 1538-1877 (CRO)
BT 157.?, 1600, 1604, 1607-10, 1613-15, 1617-19, 1624-26, 1628-29, 1635, 1658, 1663-66, 1668-76, 1679-84, 1691, 1695, 1702, 1706, 1708-09, 1712, 1714-15, 1723-25, 1727-1867, 1877-81 (+ index CB 1877-81) (CRO)
Cop 1538-1622 (Chester City Lib); M 1813-37 (NCMI); M 1668-76, 1727-1837 (CMI)
Cop (Mf) C 1538-1857, M 1538-1907, B 1538-1877 (CRO, Manchester Local Hist Lib)

WARRINGTON St Elphin ancient parish in Lancashire (with several daughter parishes), transferred to Cheshire, 1974 *see* Lancashire NIPR

WAVERTON St Peter (720) [Broxton Hundred; Great Boughton Union 1837-71, Tarvin Union 1871-1930]
OR C 1582-1863, M 1582-1837, Banns 1845-1960, B 1582-1966 (CRO)
BT 1599-1601, 1604-05, 1608-11, 1613-14, 1616-18, 1623-25, 1627, 1629-33, 1639-41, 1666, 1668-69, 1671-77, 1679-85, 1690-92, 1694-1751, 1753-54, 1756-1839, 1845-60, 1863-89 (+ index CB 1873-89) (CRO)
Cop 1582-1695 (Chester AS); M 1701-1837 (CMI)
Cop (Mf) C 1582-1863, M 1582-1837, B 1582-1966 (CRO, Manchester Local Hist Lib)

WAVERTON near Egg Bridge (Presbyterian) (K 1928)

WAVERTON near Egg Bridge, Huxley (Wesleyan Methodist) b 1842, *fl.*1978

WAVERTON (Wesleyan Methodist) (K 1928)

WAVERTON (Wesleyan Methodist) (K 1928)

WAVERTON (Baptist) (K 1928)

WAVERTON (Primitive Methodist) (K 1928)

WAVERTON Acton (Wesleyan Methodist) (K 1928)

WEAVER township in Middlewich (196)

WEAVERHAM St Mary (2,321) [Eddisbury Hundred; Northwich Union]
OR CMB 1576-1618, CM 1697+, B 1678+ (Inc)
BT 1579, 1610-12, 1614, 1617, 1621-23, 1625, 1627-30, 1637?, 1639, 1658, 1663, 1665-66, 1668-76, 1678-85, 1690-1703, 1706-39, 1741-44, 1746-89, 1791-1878, 1891-1925 (+ index CB 1873-78, 1892) (CRO)
Cop M 1577-1837 (BT & OR) (Ts I CRO); M 1700-1900 (MCMI); M 1576-1837 (NCMI); M 1714-28, 1754-1837 (CMI)

WEAVERHAM St Bede (Roman Catholic) f 1950

WERNETH *see* **COMPSTALL St Paul**

WERVIN township in Chester St Oswald (64)

WESTON by CREWE All Saints (401) township in Wybunbury, created a parish in 1841
OR CMB 1843+ (Inc)
BT 1843-76 (+ index C 1873-76) (CRO)

WESTON by CREWE (Wesleyan Methodist) (K 1928)

WESTON by CREWE (Primitive Methodist) (K 1928)

WESTON by CREWE Charlton (Primitive Methodist) (K 1928)

WESTON by RUNCORN St John the Evangelist (532) township in Runcorn [Bucklow Hundred; Runcorn Union]
OR C 1914-54, M 1924-80 (CRO)

WESTON by RUNCORN (Wesleyan Methodist) f 1832, b 1851, closed 1970
OR C 1876-1970, M 1928-70 (CRO)

WESTON POINT Christ Church chapelry in Weston by Runcorn
OR C 1843-1906 (CRO); M 1953+ (Inc)
BT 1843-82 (+ index C 1873-82) (CRO)

WESTON POINT (Wesleyan Methodist) b 1872, closed 1970
OR C 1872-1907 (CRO)

WETTENHALL St David (272) chapelry in Over, created a parish in 1720 [Eddisbury Hundred; Nantwich Union]
OR C 1824-67 (CRO); MB 1824+ (Inc)
BT 1824-50, 1855-64 (CRO)
Cop (Mf) C 1824-67 (CRO)

WETTENHALL (Primitive Methodist) b 1861 (K 1928)

WETTENHALL (Wesleyan Methodist) b 1901 (K 1928)

WHALEY township in Taxal (403)

WHALEY BRIDGE *see* **TAXAL**

WHARTON Christ Church (1,060) township in Davenham, created a parish in 1860
OR C 1843-1931, M 1850-1947, B 1843-1927 (CRO)
BT 1851-95 (+ index CB 1873-92) (CRO)

WHATCROFT township in Davenham (50)

WHEELOCK Christ Church (440) township in Sandbach, created a parish in 1840
OR C 1843-1902, M 1862-1924, B 1843-1926 (CRO)
BT 1843-46, 1848, 1851-67 (CRO)
Cop (Mf) C 1843-1902, M 1862-1924, B 1843-1926 (CRO)

WHEELOCK (Independent) f 1824 (K 1928)
OR With Ch Sec

WHEELOCK (Primitive Methodist) b 1868, closed 1940s

WHEELOCK (Wesleyan Methodist) (Lewis 1831) reb 1874 (K 1928)

WHEELOCK (Baptist) (K 1928)

WHITBY or WHITBY LOCKS St Thomas (234) township in Ellesmere Port, Eastham (part in Stoke) temporary church b 1909
OR C 1921-73, M 1960-88 (CRO)

WHITCHURCH St Alkmund (5,819) [mostly North Bradford Hundred, Shropshire, but Marbury chapelry in Nantwich Hundred, Cheshire] *see* Shropshire NIPR

WHITEGATE St Mary (909) chapelry in Over, created a parish in 1542, united to Little Budworth, 1971 [Eddisbury Hundred; Northwich Union]
OR C 1565-1932, M 1565-1942, Banns 1754-1812, B 1565-1951 (CRO)
BT 1576, 1600, 1604, 1607-09, 1611-15, 1617-20, 1622?, 1623, 1625-26, 1628-30, 1633-37, 1639, 1641, 1658-60, 1664-66, 1668-76, 1679-85, 1688-90, 1692-1738, 1740-50, 1752-1853, 1892-1911 (CRO)
Cop 1565-1837 (Ts I CRO); M 1700-1900 (MCMI); M 1813-37 (NCMI); M 1701-1837 (CMI)
Cop (Mf) C 1565-1932, M 1565-1942, Banns 1754-1812, B 1565-1951 (CRO, Manchester Local Hist Lib); C 1702-1834, M 1702-04, 1736-1813, B 1702-08, 1736-1812 (SG)

WHITEGATE Marton (Wesleyan Methodist) b 1878, *fl.* 1978

WHITLEY, HIGHER township in Great Budworth (283)

WHITLEY, LOWER St Luke (237) township in Great Budworth, created a parish in 1824
OR C 1777-1949, M 1847-1983 (CRO)
BT 1847-50 (CRO)
Cop M 1847-1900 (MCMI)
Cop (Mf) C 1777-1869 (CRO, Manchester Local Hist Lib)

WHITLEY, LOWER Cemetery (Society of Friends) (K 1928)

WHITLEY, LOWER (Wesleyan Methodist) (Lewis 1831) (K 1928)

WIDNES St Ambrose, WIDNES St John, WIDNES St Mary and WIDNES St Paul chapelries in Lancashire, transferred to Cheshire, 1974 *see* Lancashire NIPR

WIGLAND township in Malpas (265)

WILDBOARCLOUGH St Saviour (476) township in Prestbury, created a parish in 1904
OR CM 1904+ (Inc)

WILLASTON Christ Church (276) township in Neston, created a parish in 1865
OR C 1865-1944, M 1865-1944, B 1865-1933 (CRO)
BT 1892-94 (CRO)
Cop (Mf) C 1865-1902, M 1865-1924, B 1865-1933 (CRO)

WILLASTON (Primitive Methodist) b 1889 (K 1928)

WILLASTON township in Nantwich (99)

WILLASTON township in Wybunbury (122)

WILLINGTON extra-parochial place, incorporated in Kelsall, 1968 [Eddisbury Hundred; Great Boughton Union 1837-71, Tarvin Union 1871-1930] (115)

WILLINGTON (United Methodist) b 1823, reb 1865, *fl.*1958
OR C 1893-1932 (CRO)

WILMSLOW Cemetery (opened 1907; 6½ acres)

WILMSLOW St Bartholomew (4,296) [Macclesfield Hundred; Altrincham Union 1836-95, Bucklow Union 1895-1930]
OR C 1558-1877, M 1558-1863, Banns 1754-1813, 1819-45, B 1558-1882 (CRO)
BT 1599, 1605, 1608, 1610, 1617, 1620-23, 1625, 1627-29, 1631-37, 1639, 1641, 1661, 1663-85, 1687-1704, 1706-1811, 1813-23, 1825-38, 1855-59 (CRO)
Cop C 1559-1808, M 1562-1793, B 1588-1819 (Chester AS); CMB 1558-1652 (Ms I CRO); CM 1692-1740, B 1692-1734 (Ms I CRO); M 1558-71, 1692-1837 (NCMI); M 1706-15, 1756-64, 1780-89, 1799-1811 (CMI)
Cop (Mf) C 1558-1877, M 1558-1887, B 1558-1902 (CRO, Wilmslow Lib, Manchester Local Hist Lib); C 1558-1652, 1693-1741, 1779-1812, M 1558-1652, 1693-1812, 1837-47, B 1558-1652, 1692-1734 (SG)

WILMSLOW Dean Row Chapel (Presbyterian, later Unitarian) f 1672 b 1694
OR ZC 1749-1980, DB 1751, 1776-1857, Graves 1897-1934 (CRO) (this register was lost for many years and recovered in the mid-twentieth century)

WILMSLOW Lende End (Wesleyan Methodist) f 1807
OR ZC 1796-1837 (PRO: RG 4/194)
Cop (Mf) ZC 1796-1837 (CRO, SLC)

WILMSLOW Dean Row (Wesleyan Methodist: Stockport Trinity Circuit) f 1799 b 1849 (K 1928)
OR ZC 1807-37 (PRO: RG 4/2154)
Cop (Mf) ZC 1807-37 (CRO, SLC)

WILMSLOW Water Lane, Morley (Wesleyan Methodist: Stockport Circuit) f 1798 b 1884 (K 1928)

WILMSLOW Pownall Fee, Styal (Unitarian) f 1824, *fl.* 1975
OR ZC 1833-36 (PRO: RG 4/1104); C 1840-91, M 1840-90 (CRO)
Cop (Mf) ZC 1833-36 (CRO, SLC)

WILMSLOW (Independent) (Lewis 1831)

WILMSLOW Hough (Wesleyan Methodist: Alderley Edge Circuit) b 1838
OR C 1854-1984 (CRO)

WILMSLOW Lindow (United Methodist) b 1839 (K 1928)

WILMSLOW Alderley Edge (Wesleyan Methodist) b 1863 (K 1928)

WILMSLOW Meeting House, Morley (Society of Friends) f 17th century (K 1928)
OR (Morley Monthly Meeting later Cheshire Monthly Meeting) Z 1654-1830, M 1654-1831, B 1654-1776 (PRO: RG 6/96, 157, 181, 213, 1036, 1398) see also Cheshire Quaker Registers
BT 1865-66 (CRO)
Cop Z 1654-1830, M 1654-1831, B 1654-1776 (CRO, SLC)

WILMSLOW Hawthorn Street, Bollin Fee (Wesleyan Methodist) b 1870 (K 1928)

WILMSLOW Sacred Heart and St Teresa, Green Lane, Morley (Roman Catholic) f 1875 b 1913 (K 1928)

WILMSLOW Union Chapel, Brook Lane, Alderley Edge (Baptist) b 1900 (K 1928)

WILMSLOW Styal (Wesleyan Methodist) (K 1928)

WILMSLOW Meeting House, Altrincham Road (Society of Friends) (K 1928)
OR see Cheshire Quaker Registers

WIMBOLDSLEY township in Middlewich (102)

WINCHAM township in Great Budworth (589)

WINCLE St Michael chapelry in Prestbury, created a parish in 1725, united to Wildboar Clough, 1973
OR C 1803-75, B 1803-1925 (CRO); M 1837+ (Inc)
BT 1813-24, 1826-72 (CRO)
Cop C 1803-75, B 1803-1925 (CRO)

WINCLE Allgreave (Wesleyan Methodist) b 1871 (K 1928)

WINNINGTON township in Great Budworth (256)

WINSFORD Christ Church, High Street chapelry in Over
OR C dating from 1844 lost, no MB
BT 1844-54 (CRO)

WINSFORD Swanlow Lane (Independent, later United Reformed Church) b 1814, *fl.* 1991

WINSFORD Chapel Road later (1885) Winsford Hall, Wharton (Wesleyan Methodist) b 1822, reb 1885, closed 1972
OR C 1877-1919 (Circuit), C 1838-1972 (Chapel), M 1904-71 (CRO)

WINSFORD Bethesda Chapel later (1972) **Trinity**, Crook Lane later (1865) Gravel Lane later called Station Road, Wharton (Primitive Methodist) f 1835, reb 1865, 1893
OR C 1901-19 (CRO)

WINSFORD St Paul's Chapel, Over Lane later called High Street (United Methodist) b 1836, reb 1877, closed 1977
OR C 1868-1924, M 1921-77 (CRO)

WINSFORD Central Chapel, Chapel Street later (1871) Over Lane later called High Street (Primitive Methodist) b 1842, closed 1976, reopened as **St Andrew**, 1977
OR C 1861-1976, M 1959-70 (CRO)

WINSFORD Station Road later (1926) Crook Lane, Wharton (United Methodist) b 1860, closed 1972
OR C 1904-72, M 1938-70 (CRO)

WINSFORD Swanlow Lane (Wesleyan Methodist) b 1861 (K 1928)

WINSFORD Chester Road (Primitive Methodist) b 1876, *fl.*1964

WINSFORD High Street (Wesleyan Methodist) b 1883 (K 1928)

WINSFORD Meadow Bank (Primitive Methodist) b 1897, *fl.*1951

WINSFORD Weaver (United Methodist) (K 1928)

WINSFORD Swanlow (Wesleyan Methodist) (K 1928)

WINSFORD St Joseph, Ways Green (Roman Catholic) f 1949

WINWICK St Oswald ancient parish in Lancashire, transferred to Cheshire, 1974
see Lancashire NIPR

WIRSWALL township in Whitchurch (83)

WISTASTON St Mary (350) [Nantwich Hundred; Nantwich Union]
OR C 1572-1936, M 1572-1985, Banns 1755-1812, 1847-60, 1873-1987, B 1572-1945 (CRO)
BT 1593, 1605, 1607-08, 1610, 1613-14, 1617, 1620, 1622-24, 1626-30, 1632-37, 1639, 1641, 1653-60, 1662-68, 1670-72, 1674-82, 1684-85, 1688-90, 1692-1715, 1717-35, 1737-1830, 1872-82 (+ index C 1873-82) (CRO)
Cop C 1593-1700, M 1593-1700, B 1605-1700 (Chester City Lib); M 1743-1837 (NCMI); M 1675-80, 1695-1837 (CMI)
Cop (Mf) C 1572-1936, M 1572-1929, B 1572-1945 (CRO, Manchester Local Hist Lib)

WISTASTON (Methodist) b 1945, reb 1967

WITHINGTON, LOWER township in Prestbury (584)

WITHINGTON, OLD township in Prestbury (191)

WITTON chapelry in Great Budworth, created a parish in 1723 as **NORTHWICH St Helen** (q.v.) (2,912)

WOODBANK township in Shotwick (51)

WOODCHURCH Holy Cross (929) [Wirral Hundred; Wirral Union]
OR C 1571-1945, M 1571-1951, Banns 1823-72, 1923-58, B 1580-1913 (CRO)
BT 1581, 1586, 1588, 1596, 1600, 1604-05, 1607, 1609-10, 1615, 1617-19, 1621-24, 1626-27, 1630, 1632, 1634, 1636, 1638, 1642, 1658-60, 1666, 1668-70, 1672-76, 1679-82, 1684, 1690-91, 1693, 1695-97, 1699-1739, 1741-54, 1756-1826, 1829-37, 1855-56, 1858-94 (+ index CB 1873-91) (CRO)
Cop 1571-1703 (Ms CRO); 1571-1840 (Ts CRO, SG); C 1622-93, M 1600-93, B 1606-93 (Chester City Lib); M 1706-17, 1801-37 (CMI)
Cop (Mf) C 1571-1945, M 1571-1930, B 1571-1913 (CRO, Wirral Archives, Manchester Local Hist Lib)

WOODCHURCH Methodist Chapel f 1957, b 1963

WOODCOTT township in Wrenbury (30)

WOODFORD Christ Church (403) township in Prestbury, created a parish in 1873
OR C 1842-1926, M 1874-1935, B 1848-1922 (CRO)
BT 1842, 1844-46, 1848, 1850, 1852, 1854-66, 1891-92 (CRO)

WOODHEAD St James created a parish in 1724 from Mottram in Longendale
OR C 1782-1981, M 1856-1960, Banns 1854-1921, B 1782-1992 (CRO)
BT 1816-23, 1825-41, 1843-67 (CRO)
Cop 1780-1812 (Index, CRO)
Cop (Mf) CB 1782-1812 (CRO)

WOODHEAD (Calvinist Methodist) (Lewis 1831)

WOOLSTANWOOD township in Nantwich (70)

WORLESTON St Oswald (367) township in Acton, created a parish in 1873
OR CMB 1872+ (Inc)
BT 1873-82 (+ index CB 1873-82) (CRO)

WORLESTON Poole (Wesleyan Methodist) b 1834 (K 1928)

WORLESTON (United Methodist) b 1891, closed 1969

WORLESTON Aston juxta Mondrum (United Methodist) (K 1928)

WORLESTON Cholmondeston (Wesleyan Methodist) (K 1928)

WORTH township in Prestbury, united to Poynton, 1745 (490)

WRENBURY St Margaret (903) chapelry in Acton, created a parish in 1730
OR C 1593-1882, M 1593-1965, Banns 1757-1812, 1826-1963, B 1593-1918 (CRO)
BT 1593, 1599-1600, 1604?, 1605-14, 1616, 1620-24, 1626-28, 1630-33, 1636-41, 1658-85, 1693-95, 1697-1833, 1835-37, 1840-42, 1878-81 (+ index CB 1878-81) (CRO)
Cop 1599-1799 (Chester City Lib); Extr 1593-1812 (Nantwich Lib, SG); M 1790-1804, 1811-33 (CMI)
Cop (Mf) C 1593-1882, M 1593-1884, B 1593-1855 (CRO, Manchester Local Hist Lib)

WRENBURY Dodd's Green (Wesleyan Methodist) b 1835 (K 1928)

WRENBURY Sound (United Methodist) b 1838 (K 1928)

WRENBURY Wrenbury Heath (Primitive Methodist) b 1848, closed 1918

WRENBURY Aston (Wesleyan Methodist) b 1866 (K 1928)

WRENBURY Sound (Primitive Methodist) b 1875, *fl.*1955

WREXHAM Board of Guardians (Wrexham was in Denbighshire, but the Poor Law Union covered some Cheshire parishes)
OR ZD 1886-1914 (Clwyd RO)

WYBUNBURY St Chad (4,193) [Nantwich Hundred; Nantwich Union]
OR C 1558-1957, M 1558-1958, Banns 1754-87, 1802-72, 1885-1965, B 1558-1962 (CRO)
BT 1600, 1603, 1607-08, 1611, 1614-15, 1617-18, 1622-24, 1627-29, 1631-33, 1636-39, 1640 (part), 1658-85, 1687-1715, 1717-1880 (+ index CB 1873-80) (CRO)
Cop 1600-41, 1660-1799 (Chester City Lib); M 1813-37 (NCMI); M 1754-1800, 1812, 1834-37 (CMI)
Cop (Mf) C 1558-1957, M 1558-1958, B 1558-1962 (CRO, Manchester Local Hist Lib)

WYBUNBURY Wesley Place Chapel (Wesleyan Methodist) b 1817, reb 1831, 1864
OR M 1925-69 (CRO)

WYBUNBURY Shavington cum Gresty (United Methodist) f 1835, b 1886, closed 1936
OR C 1904-36 (CRO)

WYBUNBURY Englesea Brook Chapel, Weston (Methodist)
OR B 1842-1957

WYBUNBURY Liverpool Road, Hough (Primitive Methodist) b 1860, closed 1987
OR C 1854-1960 (Chester RO); M 1909-81 (CRO)

WYBUNBURY Mount Pleasant Chapel, Weston (Primitive Methodist) b 1854, closed 1959

WYBUNBURY Crewe Road, Hatherton (Primitive Methodist) b 1864, *fl.*1960

WYBUNBURY Willaston (Wesleyan Methodist) b 1864 (K 1928)

WYBUNBURY Rope Lane Chapel, Shavington cum Gresty (Primitive Methodist) b 1869, closed 1967
OR M 1926-55 (CRO)

WYBUNBURY Free Gospel Chapel, Shavington cum Gresty b 1871 (K 1928)

WYBUNBURY Willaston (Primitive Methodist) b 1875 (K 1928)

WYBUNBURY Shavington cum Gresty (Wesleyan Methodist) b 1876 (K 1928)

WYBUNBURY Blakenhall (Wesleyan Methodist) b 1900 (K 1928)

WYBUNBURY Hatherton (Wesleyan Methodist) b 1900 (K 1928)

WYBUNBURY Centenary Chapel, Stapeley (Primitive Methodist) b 1908 (K 1928)

WYCHOUGH township in Malpas (35)

WYTHENSHAWE St Richard of Chichester created a parish in 1971 from Benchill

WYTHENSHAWE The William Temple Church created a parish in 1963 from Benchill, Northenden and Stockport

YEARDSLEY cum WHALLEY township in Taxal